GUCCI ON THE GINZA

Japan's *NEW* Consumer Generation

GUCCI ON THE GINZA

JAPAN'S *NEW* CONSUMER GENERATION

GEORGE FIELDS

KODANSHA INTERNATIONAL
Tokyo and New York

Distributed in the United States by Kodansha International/USA Ltd., 114 Fifth Avenue, New York, New York, 10011.
Published by Kodansha International Ltd., 2-2, Otowa 1-chome, Bunkyo-ku, Tokyo 112, and Kodansha International/USA Ltd., 114 Fifth Avenue, New York, 10011.

First Kodansha International printing, 1989.

This edition is published by arrangement with the original publisher, The Japan Times, Ltd. Published in Japan under the title *The Japanese Market Culture.*

Gucci is a registered trademark of GUCCI O GUCCI SPO

Library of Congress Cataloging-in-Publication Data

Fields, George.
    [Japanese market culture]
    Gucci on the Ginza: Japan's new consumer generation / George Fields.
       p.   cm
    "Published in Japan under the title The Japanese market culture"—T.p. verso.
    1. Consumers—Japan—Attitudes.
2. Marketing—Japan.   3. Investments, Foreign—Japan
4. Japan—Social life and customs—1945– I. Title.
HC465.C8F54 1989 658. 8' 342' 0952—do19 88-46050
ISBN 0-87011-927-3 (U.S.)

CONTENTS

INTRODUCTION

THIS BOOK is about continuity and change. In my 1982 book, *From Bonsai to Levi's*, I was primarily concerned with the former, arguing that despite visible "Westernization," many values affecting this market remained staunchly Japanese. The message was that the foreign marketer could ignore this detail at his own peril. Since then, the phrase "global marketing" has become fashionable in some quarters and marketers have joined separate camps, for and against. There is, however, no division in the perception that certain global trends will affect one's own market at an unprecedented pace. Certainly, a killing can be made by spotting early change, but there is, of course, a very big difference between mere fashion and a permanent shift. Continuity, of course, does not imply permanency. When basic values are concerned, short of a social upheaval, changes are rarely effected overnight and tend to evolve slowly.

Yet recent events do suggest an upheaval in the Japanese market. Certainly the happenings of the past few years have had an impact far exceeding those over the 20 years or so since the Tokyo Olympics in 1964. But why? Compared with the arrival of Perry's black ships, the collapse of the long shogun reign, flirtations with Western ideologies such as liberalism and Marxism, the great depression, and, of course, the defeat in a catastrophic war and the oil shock, the current trade-induced problems seem almost benign. Nevertheless, traumatic as preceding events were, Japanese values that developed during the country's long periods of isolation have been largely left intact. On the other hand, various factors converging now have long-term implications that affect the basic culture.

In each of the past four years, the Japanese media have focused on major phenomena, discussing and dissecting them *ad nauseam*. The first was the evolving role of women, triggered by the United Nation's declaration of a "Woman's Year" which ushered in Japan's "Equal Opportunities in Employment Act." With typical concern for what others think, the government and the powerful employers' associations decided that Japan must not appear to be apathetic on the issue when compared to the West. While the act was more symbolic than substantive, a remarkable debate ensued, with an avalanche of letters to the press by women questioning society's traditional perception of the role of the sexes. While the legislation itself may have been mostly window dressing, taken together with macro-economic forces which are drawing an increasing number of women into the work force, organic changes are clearly under way.

Then came the super buzzword—*shinjinrui* (literally, "the new human species")—referring to the new generation of young. It is claimed that in 1986 this word was used more than any other in the media. The next year brought *endaka* (the high yen) and *kokusaika* (internationalization), the two being related in the short-term. Initially, all the debate was on macro-economic or institutional aspects. However, it quickly dawned on many segments of Japanese society that accommodating global free trade rules isn't just a question of reorganizing production or restructuring employment, but that it involves changes in the market culture, in both consumer and corporate values. For the latter, it is ironic that the West has only just become accustomed to Japanese managerial philosophies just at the time these are about to change for the Japanese!

When I compiled my original material for this book in May 1988, the new buzz words were *naiju* (domestic demand), *nyū ritchi* (the new rich), and NICs (the Newly Industrialized Countries) - the last modified since to NIES, the "E" standing for "Economies" replacing the "C" for "Countries," because of the objection raised that Hong Kong, a member of this group, was not a country. As I re-edit the material in December 1988, another buzz word, *"kakusa,"* has entered the fray. The word, which translates literally as "difference in quality," is now used to signify concern for a society that will no longer be comfortably considered as dominantly middle-class and is thus a spin-off from, or a quick follow-up on, *nyū ritchi*.

Of the somewhat earlier buzz words, unlike *shinjinrui,* "internationalization" has remained hot without any indication of a cool off. This is not surprising, as most of the other buzz words spring from phenomena which are a consequence of "internationalization."

While the media may have preferred a thorough exploration of one subject at a time, as they are prone to do, the issues are far too complex for this to be possible. It is not any single factor but the convergence of many that is creating havoc with the tranquility of a society that has managed—and preferred—to live for a long time with its self-imposed values. Contrary to the belief by some in the West, it is not that the Japanese have largely ignored foreign values. In fact, they have always been fascinated with them and study them very carefully. But on the whole, they have managed to adapt rather than absorb these values in the course of modernizing. The past few years suggest that it is going to be difficult to sustain this balancing act.

It is therefore not surprising that my various observations in print have dealt with the impact of these factors on the market. Writing on the market often focuses on transitory phenomenon such as hit products, or is simply descriptive and generally only of short-term interest, primarily to the practitioner. However, I have always subscribed to the truism, "Markets are people and people are markets." So, when my articles and columns were organized by category, to me, a picture of the Japanese people and the market in transition seemed to emerge via attitudes and behavior of the consumer and the marketer.

This book attempts to bring that picture into closer focus. Part I deals with the hang-ups and other idiosyncracies of the generations that make up the various segments of the Japanese market. Part II is largely concerned with matters that often puzzle the visitor, in the systems of communication and matters of perception. The discourse on semantics may be of interest to the advertising specialist, but can be safely skipped by others. Part III discusses the Japanese claim to uniqueness, which provided amusing material in the early days, but which is becoming an irritant as Japan asserts its role in the international community. Part IV looks at the emerging role of a "new" Japanese consumer. While both Japan and most of the West belong to the "capitalist camp," each positions the consumer differently. The "wakening" of the Japanese consumer brings the Japanese position closer to the West, but not without shaking up the existing infrastructure. The chapters in Part V are, on the whole, recent and, not surprisingly, they address change—some basic, some peripheral—but in all cases, they attempt to explain the new forces on the market. Part VI is my entry into the long-standing debate on global marketing and a perspective on the synthesis of internationalization Japanese-style. By sheer coincidence, several of my latest contributions in print serve as the basis for the concluding section.

Dynamic forces shape the new Japanese market. My hope is that the reader, traversing through the wake, will discover a greater feeling for change within the cultural framework. In some small way, perhaps my observations will be useful in the reader's personal approach to the market.

GEORGE FIELDS

Tokyo, Japan
December, 1988

GUCCI ON THE GINZA

PART ONE

MacArthur's Children, The Tokyo Olympians, And The *Shinjinrui*

THE BALL GAME WAS NOT THE POINT

IT WAS IN 1984, just one year before the word *shinjinrui* (literally, "a new species of person") became a phenomenal buzz word, that I found a way to explain the significance of the generation change that was overtaking Japan and of why the older generation was more than usually concerned about the younger generation. More precisely, somebody else, an eminent Japanese, provided me with the right example.

After all, most societies have been concerned about the up-and-coming generation, often lamenting that the youth are in the process of destroying basic values. Hackneyed examples from the time of the pyramids and Socrates are trotted out. Japanese were of course not unique in suffering the traumas of the Second World War, and since there was no combat on their main island, the last battle being fought in Okinawa, a strong case could be made that the war had affected European countries more profoundly than Japan. This may explain why the issue of the generations emerged much earlier in Germany, the ally in Japan's defeat. The destruction of the Third Reich shook German values much more profoundly than the disbanding of the zaibatsu conglomerates and the changing of the guard in Japan.

Typically, change was imposed from outside, symbolized in the name of the conqueror, MacArthur. More than forty years after the war, not many senior Japanese feel particularly obligated to uphold some of the changes effected. When it suits them, certain aspects are upheld, such as the peace constitution, which prevents them from gaining a sharp increase in the defense budget. When it is awkward—as exemplified by the incredible protection afforded to farmers' land ownership via special tax laws, exacerbating the acute shortage in residential space—it can be gleefully pointed out that the problem stems from occupation "reforms." German change came internally, with considerable spiritual agonizing. Japanese change was simply imposed from outside.

The relevance of the MacArthur period to the current fear of the new generation became clear to me at a Japanese conference at which I was the opening speaker. The conference was for those in the textile and fashion industry and was held at a hot-spring resort about one hour outside of the port city of Kobe. I was talking about changes in the Japanese consumer market as seen from "foreign" eyes; it was a typically Western speech, too structured, too pat. The following speaker's style, full of personal reminiscences and anecdotes with well-known names, made my speech eminently forgettable. (It was at this conference that I decided to change my speaking style for a Japanese audience and it seems to have worked.)

The speaker was Masahiro Shinoda, one of Japan's best known film directors. Shinoda was then in his early fifties, I guess, and his talk revolved around his latest hit film *Setouchi Shōnen Yakyū-dan* [The Setouchi Little-League Team], which is known in English as *MacArthur's Children*. The film was made even more memorable by being the last film made by the beautiful young actress Masako Natsume before she succumbed to leukemia. While his remarks did speak of the passing of Natsume with some feeling, capturing the audience emotionally, when it came to the film, he went on to emphasize what it was not.

The film's plot, simply put, was about the arrival of the occupation forces in a small Japanese village and how they and the concept of democracy they brought were viewed through the eyes of a class of junior high-school boys. They scrape and save and get hand-me-down baseball equipment to wage a baseball match with a group of American GIs, which constitutes the climax of the film and hence the title. The film, however, was most definitely not about baseball. Nor was it about the democratizing of Japan. It was about the trauma of receiving an alien presence in a completely isolated Japanese community. Indeed, the "aliens" could have been from Mars as far as the villagers were concerned. The visual impact was strengthened by Glen Miller's music—especially "In the Mood"—coming through on the soundtrack.

Since I am only a few years older, and since I was in Tokyo when the Second World War ended, I can claim to be of Shinoda's generation, despite the fact that I headed toward Australia, in a troop transport ship, shortly afterward. The sound of Glen Miller did indeed herald an outside world with an amazing difference. Unfortunately, for those who were on the other end of the combat, the film may have had certain elements that conveyed the perception of the Japanese as "victims" and the Americans as trespassers a little too strongly. For example, there was the fine father who was suddenly taken away by burly American MPs, in front of his shocked family, as a class-B war criminal. Later the sad news of his execution reached the hamlet, and somehow the audience is made to feel that an atrocity is committed by the war-crimes court.

Still, the film was a great cultural commentary, and the fact that it was made in 1984, so long after the ending of World War II, seems significant. It was right that it was taken to the United States, probably shown in the art-theater circuit. However, the original title would have been clearly inappropriate in English, indicating merely a Japanese version of "Good Luck Bears!" Whoever gave the film its English title, *MacArthur's Children,* was a genius. MacArthur's children are now in Japan's driver's seat as politicians, government officials, corporate executives, etc. They maintain a complex set of attitudes toward the world outside and are ambivalent toward cultural "contamination." In the current climate of trade tension, their love-hate feelings toward the United States are becoming increasingly apparent. But what of the children of MacArthur's children?

Japan Opened with the Tokyo Olympics, Not with Commodore Perry

I RETURNED TO JAPAN after an absence of some 15 years in 1960 and then again in 1962, and 1964. In each case, I made relatively short stays of from 4 to 6 weeks, all of which were occasions of considerable emotional self-evaluation of my cultural identity. The 1964 visit finally triggered my return to Japan in the following year, on business. It was the year of the Olympics, but my visit occurred before that momentous event, in the first two months of the year. I was on a survey mission sponsored by the Australian National Travel Association, and we looked at the potential outward-bound traveler market from Japan.

There was none, if we excluded the non-casual travelers such as businessmen with the mission to export, scholars, journalists, students, etc., all with a mission to contribute to Japanese society by bringing something back, be it export income, knowledge, or skills. In this sense, nothing had changed from the Meiji era—starting in 1868—when the government made the decision to "open" the Japanese shores to foreign influences. Selected elite personages were sent forth to the West during the Meiji era in order to propel Japan into the modern world, but this was in order to advance technology to protect Japan from the outside, and fundamental societal values from the feudal era were kept intact.

Most Japanese travelers in 1964 had to justify their overseas trips before they could get a passport. True, in that year, the reason for this was economic rather than political and did not involve the kind of restriction imposed on personal movement by Iron Curtain countries. Japan had been running a chronic trade deficit, and the government was obsessed with this problem. So even when the odd person who traveled for pleasure was granted a passport, his foreign-exchange allowance was hardly adequate for the sort of junkets that are common now. Who could have predicted an outflow of more than 6 million, predicted to be 10 million in the near future, with virtually no limitation on the currency that could be taken out.

However, there was another big inhibitor. To the average Japanese traveler, the outside world was an inhospitable place, with memories of World War II still lingering, especially in Australia and Southeast Asia. But all of that seemed to change with the Tokyo Olympics, which also coincided with the television era in many parts of the world. Here was Japan seen in a new light. The world was impressed with the superb organization and spectacle. Visitors were impressed with the charm of the Japanese people, and became instant opponents of maintaining a silly war-generated stereotypical view of the Japanese—even in Australia where the Japanese were, by and large till then, considered to be subhuman. Japanese who were youths at that time speak of the tremendous impact of the many young foreign athletes who poured in. So I happened to return at a time of considerable social transformation and a significant break in Japan's cultural insularity. It is really only a little over twenty years since Japan first started to become engaged in what they call "internationalization''—more on that later—and Japan has actually come a remarkable way since, contrary to many a view held in the West.

The Sun Tribe: A Transition from MacArthur's Children

BUT THERE WAS A GAP in my knowledge on the species that was engendered by MacArthur's children. Although I shared my childhood with MacArthur's children, I was absent from Japan in a period in which they had to cope with the grim conditions that prevailed just after World War II. This gap could have been filled to a certain extent by Japanese films of that period. The ones that I saw, however, tended to be those of high artistic merit; there was also a genre of film I scorned from pure intellectual snobbery that featured Japanese youth, a sad admission for a so-called student of Japanese culture. A serious void has been filled recently with a vertiable orgy of retrospective films on television starring the actor Yūjirō Ishihara.

The comments on the rough international waters and on trade issues that directly concerned Japan were temporarily ignored by the Japanese media in the summer of 1987. The popular media were obsessed with the passing of Yūjirō Ishihara at age 52. He was a pre-Olympic Tokyoite, and, by generation, one of MacArthur's children. Noted intellectuals weighed in with dissertations on the significance of Yūjirō to the post—World War II generation. His elder brother, the charismatic parliamentarian Shintarō—who became Minister of Transportation soon after his brother's death, with the formation of the Takeshita cabinet—was featured over and over again, giving personal reminiscences of the deceased star. It was the movie based on his award-winning novel, *Taiyō no kisetsu* [Seasons in the Sun], that pushed Yūjirō into stardom and provided the label *taiyōzoku* (the sun tribe) for the new generation.

The passing of great personalities can remind one of significant stages in one's own life. In 1987, the death of Fred Astaire brought back memories of my childhood in the Tokyo immediately preceding World War II, where I was mesmerized by the silver screen lit up by him and his partner, Ginger Rogers, before the lights went out on the Ginza. Americans of various generations have been affected: perhaps by the passing of Valentino, in an earlier period, and certainly in more recent times by Dean, Presley, Lennon, and Wayne.

"MacArthur's Children" and "Tokyo Olympians" are labels I have invented and that are not used by the Japanese; stereotyping generations is not a unique Japanese pastime. However, in Japan, the prevalent labels have been associated with the reign of the Emperor. Hence, there is the Meiji man from the period which spanned 1868 to 1912, who was respected for his nationalistic leadership qualities that brought Japan into the modern world; the Taishō man, who flourished during the short span from 1912 to 1926, who is associated with the myth that Japan flirted with democracy.

The Shōwa era was the longest reign in Japan's history, and has to be further segmented. World War II is the divider, with its *senzen-ha* (prewar faction), *senchū-ha* (midwar faction), and *sengo-ha* (postwar faction) generations.

All the designations of the Emperor's reign have symbolic importance. *Mei* in *Meiji* can mean "lightness" or "clarity" and *ji* is the second part of *seiji,* which is "politics," so the tone was set for Japan to enter the modern age and to discard away some of the legacies of feudalism, with the designation, "enlightened governance." The *Tai* of *Taishō* is "large" and *shō* is the first character for "justice," or the last character for "fairness," so the short-lived Taishō period started as that of "great justice or fairness"; it was indeed a period in which Japan flirted with democracy. *Shōwa,* having ended in its 64th year the longest in history, has a designation that is the most ironic because it could mean "enlightened peace," for an era that produced the most cataclysmic war in Japan's history.

But back to Yūjirō and the new label that came to be associated with him. While the Meiji and Taishō stereotypes could exist anyway, they belong to the past — the reign of Showa, as we have seen with its twists and turns, was spawning sub-labels. Yūjirō was perhaps the first to create one around a persona with a new attitude to life. He successfully labeled a segment of his generation the *taiyōzoku* (the sun tribe) who trumpeted their departure from the fold of MacArthur's children.

What characterized the *taiyōzoku*—and this is the "sun" part—was the optimism that was lacking in the postwar Japanese until then. Yūjirō's physical characteristics helped. He was long legged and not at all inferior, it seemed, to the American GI. Yūjirō was always a winner and couldn't give a damn about convention and was always on the side of the weak, like those heroes in Hollywood films. He did, however, retain the Japanese virtue of *giri*—loyalty to his group—and was thus a Japanese rather than a Western hero. While Japanese intellectuals were proud of the success of such films as *Rashomon, Jigokumon,* and *Tales of Ugetsu* at overseas film festivals, the box-office hits in Japan were the films of Yūjirō, which had a much less complex message, for he was no James Dean and not a rebel.

So the average Japanese person in 1987 mourned the passing of a star and realized that the days of striving to become equals to the West were over and that the Tokyo Olympians were now getting into the driver's seat. Americans were the secret role models of Japanese youth when Yūjirō's popularity was at its peak, but such a model is no longer required. Who will be the symbol of the new drivers? This is still not entirely clear. Maybe we no longer need superstars. If one does emerge, he will be very different from Yūjirō, that's for sure.

THE *SHINJINRUI:* A SPECIES WITH NO HANG-UPS

THERE IS MUCH UNCERTAINTY concerning the *shinjinrui,* since it is the first generation in modern Japanese history that is not obsessed with the menace of the outside world. While German youths are often cited in comparison, the only thing they have in common is that both of their nations were defeated in World War II. Unlike the Japanese, the German people were never artificially cut-off from their neighbors. That's why the most often used *kī wādo* (key word, i.e., Japanese for buzz word) for 1986 was *shinjinrui.* (The word is objected to by many young people as a put-down). Actually, *kī wādo* itself is a new Japanese buzz word and a list of 100 such popular words is now produced each year and revised annually thereafter. There are key characters too; a single Chinese character is chosen to connote a situation that is multidimensional (we have seen this in the previous illustrations of the designations for the emperors' eras). The Japanese penchant for symbolism is again evident. Basic to all this fuss about the *shinjinrui* is the almost paranoid fear on the part of the older generation that they may lose control and that the new values that replace the old ones may destroy the essentially Japanese qualities that are the basis of the culture's strength. (The rest of the world has heard all this before). The popularity of the *shinjinrui* among some foreign commentators actually doesn't help. The late American humorist Robert Benchley once said that you could classify people into two types: those who classified people into two types and those who didn't. These days, I have begun to classify senior Japanese businessmen into two types: those who are dismayed at the *shinjinrui* and those who are not.

Miyoji Misawa, the head of Misawa Homes, is one of the most innovative business leaders around, and he belongs to the latter. In 1984, I heard him speak at a prestigious top-management seminar run by the Japan Productivity Center. I was privileged to be the first foreign coordinator for the event, which has been taking place each year for quite some time.

Shinjinrui was yet to be a key word but Mr. Misawa stated to a startled audience that his company had two types of employees, the Japanese and the Jews. I hasten to add that the mention of the latter had absolutely no racist overtones. (A very interesting book, *The Japanese and the Jews,* had been a sleeper for the book trade a few years earlier, becoming a runaway best seller, and was a serious attempt at cross-cultural comparisons). He went on to explain that in his company, there were employees on two totally different value systems, those over 30 and those under. The latter he called the Jews, only because he thought they possessed cultural values that were different from his own. He said he had no desire to force the two cultures into the same mold and was already taking steps to incorporate a new management style for the new minority, who would eventually become the majority. We may debate whether the division is quite as drastic as Mr. Misawa suggests, but the point was well made.

This brings me to another key word—*kokusaika,* or ''internationalization''; like *shinjinrui,* it is an extremely vague and ill-defined concept. Mr. Misawa at that time could not conceive of a day when a significant minority employed by his or any Japanese company would be foreigners. But this has become an issue with the current *kokusaika* frenzy. Needless to say, foreigners will constitute another kind of *shinjinrui.* Can a Japanese corporation stomach another set of employees who are yet again different in their values? I already have this problem; there are around 12 foreigners in my company, constituting about 10 percent of the permanent work force. I'm not in the same league as Mr. Misawa as a businessman or a manager, but I too gave up quite a while ago in managing the different segments in the same way. As the saying goes, I needed this new frill to personnel management like a hole in the head.

THE *SHIN*(NEW)-*SHINJINRUI:*
A NEW PERSPECTIVE

TODAY'S *SHINJINRUI* were born in a country not at war with anybody and which counts itself as perhaps one of the most peaceful and contented of the advanced nations. As we have seen, it was not like that for their parents. August is the time for war memories, and for all of Japan to be reminded of the peace constitution. A perennial debate rages over whether government ministers should officially visit the Yasukuni Shrine, where the war dead are commemorated under Shinto rites, since the sponsoring of a religion by the government has been banned by the constitution. On the surface, we could be deceived into thinking that nothing has changed in this respect since the cessation of World War II.

Yet a survey conducted by the *Asahi Gakusei Shimbun* (a student newspaper) in 1987 revealed a startling change in attitude among Japanese junior high students. "Only" 38% thought that Japan may be at war in the future, but that is surely more than one would expect. However, we can be skeptical of such a question: the fact that it is even posed could result in a certain number saying "yes." But what was startling was that when they were asked who was most likely to be the enemy, the United States led the Soviet Union by 49% versus 41%, a response that could never have come from either MacArthur's children or the *taiyōzoku* (Sun Tribe).

The reason most often given for having to fight with the U.S. by these *shin-shinjinrui* was, not surprisingly, trade friction. The language used in the media on this issue, in both countries, is indeed riddled with battle phrases, so in that sense the result is not surprising. However, that the United States can be even imagined to be a real adversary speaks for the times and the paranoia that is gripping Japan.

If anything, much of the information on World War II published in Japan concerns the tragedies visited on the population, culminating in the atomic bomb. Japan as a victim is coming through loud and clear. More than two-thirds of the students felt that Japan was still carrying the scars of the war, and Hiroshima and Nagasaki were paramount in their consciousness. Overseas commentators, particularly the Chinese and Southeast Asians, are concerned about the seeming lack of awareness on the part of the young Japanese regarding their past role as an aggressor.

All are victims in a war, but most cultures will consider themselves more victimized by the other guy. It is not entirely fair to blame Japan for that tendency. But now the Japanese see themselves as victims of "Japan bashing" by the United States, and there is little understanding at the popular level as to why this state of affairs should have come about. The fact that the United States is not the only one that is critical of Japan's trade policies gets only small mention in the popular media. Although the number of youths who feel that the United States is the possible No. 1 enemy constitutes only a minority—49% of 38% is about 1 in 5—still, even a few years ago, such a result would have been inconceivable.

The other response to the survey strikes a more optimistic note. When asked what they would do if war broke out, the answer most often given was "run away to another safe country." Slightly over forty years ago, there were no such options. Unfortunately, they were not asked where they would escape to—presumably 1 in 5 would not say the United States, but let us not expect logic in such a survey. The fact that the United States is no longer seen as a benign big brother may not be such a bad thing if it means that the psychological dependency has now been shaken off. Without self-confidence, the reluctance to be exposed to foreign cultural values will continue.

PART TWO

COMMUNICATING WITH
THE JAPANESE CONSUMER

ALL THOSE FOREIGNERS
IN JAPANESE ADVERTISING

Questions for Which Answers are Not Expected

PROFESSOR DONALD KEENE of Columbia University once contributed a series to the *Asahi Shimbun* (a leading Japanese national daily) called "Questions Asked of Me by the Japanese." The *Asahi* drew attention to the fact that it was written in Japanese—an amazing feat for a foreigner, despite the fact that Dr. Keene was a noted Japanese scholar! Of course, most foreigners who stay in Japan, however briefly, will have had the experience of being asked things like "What do you think of Japan?" or, if male, "What do you think of Japanese girls?" The answer that was expected in both cases was (and still is), "Great!" This usually satisfies the questioner and does not lead to difficult follow-up probes such as "In what way?"

With the emergence of Japan as a super-economic power in the mid-1980s, such questions are being asked less and less frequently. There seems to have been a quantum leap in national self-consiousness in the ten years since the mid-1970s. But the attitude that often caused the Japanese to ask Dr. Keene questions like "Do you understand haiku?'' remains even today in 1988. When asked a question like this, Dr. Keene says that he is tempted to counterpose "Do you?'' — because within the question is the feeling that "no foreigner can understand things that are really Japanese,'' even if that foreigner can read *The Tale of Genji* in the original eleventh-century Japanese, which many Japanese cannot do. (Neither can many English speakers read *Beowulf* in its original late tenth-century English, if it comes to that.)

Foreigners in Japanese Advertising

It is indeed true that the haiku is a truly Japanese art form that might remain unfathomable to all but a few foreigners who have mastered the language. But then the question might be asked why so many foreigners are being used in Japanese advertising. (One presumes that if they don't know anything about Japanese culture their endorsement of a product would be useless. But one presumes wrongly.) Indeed, the frequent use of foreigners has continued to puzzle newcomers since the 1970s, and it is the question put to me most often. As awareness of Japan started to rise in the U.S. in the early 1980s, this state of affairs aroused the curiosity of U.S. newsmen, too. In 1983, CBS, in its "Evening News with Dan Rather,'' as well as the *New York Times* (in its Sunday edition), ran a feature on foreigners in Japanese advertising. The CBS version concentrated on the visual aspects, and I appeared in an interview of about a minute and a half. True to form I think, I got two lines in the *New York Times,* together with many Japanese authorities. What was striking was that my Japanese colleagues were no more coherent in their explanations than I was.

The Expected Answer: Foreigners are Fantastic

I, and, it seems, the others quoted, gave only the expected answers. They went something like this. In the land where everybody is alike, the foreigners are attention-getting with—in the early days—their blond or red hair and, of course, blue eyes. (Now blacks provide even greater exoticism). They provide glamour for fantasizing. The original argument was that the foreigners by and large do look different and thus provide the opportunity of product differentiation when used in an ad. Alas, although the argument may have been valid in the earlier days, surely it can no longer apply when there are so many foreigners in Japanese advertising.

In postwar advertising, the avalanche started with Charles Bronson. It was about the time that I returned to Japan—1965—that the Lion Dentifrice Company and Bristol Meyers changed the male toiletries market with the introduction of Vitalis hair liquid. Until then, men's hair dressing, which now accounts for the largest segment of Japanese male toiletries, was dominated by solid pomades, said to be more suitable to the stiff Japanese hair. However, the image was old-fashioned and it was time for a change, which Vitalis triggered, to be followed by others. The largest marketer of pomades at the time was Yanagiya, who was caught off guard and driven to the wall.

The company lacked funds to combat the giant Lion and the story is that it went to its advertising agency for help. The result was a staggering effort at revamping the image of an ailing brand. The old established Yanagiya brand name was dropped and the Western brand name of Mandom was introduced in a very brave (or perhaps desperate) move. The vehicle was the craggy visage of Bronson.

The advent of Bronson was in 1970. He was followed in 1972 by the French star, Alain Delon, for the fashion house, Renown; and by the late David Niven, for Mandom again in 1973. (The contrast between Bronson and Niven is striking, but the advertiser obviously was not worried because he probably felt that the foreign factor overrode any image confusions!) We were then treated by a Who's Who in Western show business, by stars who refused to appear in commercials in their own country. There was Sammy Davis Jr. for Suntory; Peter Fonda, again for Renown; Orson Welles for Nikka Whisky—the maker of *Citizen Kane* and the portrayer of Harry Lime also pushed an English-language course and continues to do so, even after his death. Sophia Loren appeared for both Honda motor bikes and Lux toilet soap. The super brat in tennis, John Mc Enroe, was in a car commercial, and Tony "Psycho" Perkins appeared for Kanebo male toiletries. The list continues and to this day shows no signs of abating.

The Rokumeikan Era in Advertising

Some Japanese started to feel that enough was enough quite early. In July 2, 1976, the following huffy comment appeared in the *Asahi* newspaper:

> For some reason, even kids and babies are crazy about these blue eyes. I am startled to see a large close-up of imbecilic expressions on a foreign woman, in broad daylight, on my T.V. screen. Commercials which are offensive to the ear keep popping up, using English, French, and something like Japanese pronounced with a physically inadequate tongue. . . .

Surely, there is no other country like this anywhere in the world! Can you imagine a Japanese appearing in a foreign commercial, spouting broken English?

What I really can't understand is why foreign stars have to be used to advertise Japanese products. In the first place, what effects can the advertiser expect by using a foreign star? Does it mean that the fact a foreigner is using it provides a guarantee for product quality?

The editorial went on. It must have seemed to the writer like the infamous Rokumeikan era, a time after the opening of Japan when the establishment went all agog about anything Western and even held a ball at which obviously uncomfortable Japanese women danced to the strains of the Viennese waltz. However, Japan appears to have matured considerably since the days of the acerbic comment, and, as has been characteristic in other aspects, the Japanese have accepted the change and absorbed its effects. So, foreign stars flood the Japanese screen, but now only newly arrived foreigners are surprised and ask why.

Just as the Rokumeikan era was one phase in Japanese cultural history, the appearances of foreign stars in Japanese advertising have gone through distinct phases and the reasons for their use are not the same over time. To start with, while the repeated claim that the Japanese culture is unique is tiresome, it is hard to find a parallel in world history of a major, advanced culture isolating itself from the rest of the world for almost 300 years, which is what Japan did under the Tokugawa shogunate. For all intents and purposes, there were no foreigners in Japan during that period.

The Foreign Menace to the Japanese Culture

In Japan's past history, foreigners have been regarded as potential invaders, and the exaggerated fear that they would lead to the destruction of the Japanese spirit—triggered by the Christian missionaries—led to the closing of Japan to the rest of the world for over two centuries. Japan opened its doors to the world under the threat of the guns of the Western blackships. *"Kurofune torai!"* ("The blackships have come!") is part of the Japanese modern vocabulary. The doors were again closed during World War II, only to be forcefully reopened by the victorious Allied forces.

Attitudes formed during the *sakoku* (Closing of the country) period still linger among the pre-Tokyo Olympians. It is difficult to imagine a modern nation in which a large segment existed for so long without a strong consciousness of the outside world. Yet the Japanese in the Tokugawa period were a highly literate race, and the cultural elite—if not the general populace—were certainly well aware of the outside world. "A frog in a well does not know of the existence of the ocean" is a favorite Japanese saying.

Thus, there was always the fear among the elite that their idyllic existence would some day come to an end. End, it did, with the emergence of Commodore Perry's black ships off the coast of Shimoda. In the long history of Japan, it was just to be expected—it took longer than usual, that is all. After all, Japan has always been under the shadow of the more "advanced" great powers—China, Korea, and Mongolia. After Perry, there were the Russians and Europeans—especially the British—as well as the new Pacific neighbor and rival, the United States.

As a menace, the foreigner has always occupied a special place in

Japanese culture. The *tengu*, a long nosed, red-faced mythological being that kept many a grizzling child quiet as the bogey man, probably had its origin in the preson of a hapless Caucasian sailor stranded on the Japanese coast. To have a tame foreigner in tow—such as Anjin-san in *Shogun*—imparted the ultimate prestige. However, until the 1970s, incredible as it seems now, with many major leaguers commanding millions of dollars in Japanese professional baseball, Japanese advertisers were not able to afford the huge salaries demanded by Western stars. The use of these stars coincided with the ascension of Japan as an economic colossus. This was phase one. The advertiser, perhaps unconsciously, was trying to project the image of himself as a world rather than a local entity—he was on equal or better terms with the best.

All that changed and we entered phase two. The xenophobia that has delayed trade liberalization and is plaguing international relationship appears to have been dissipated in the world of advertising. Thus, I believe we have entered the E.T. phase for foreigners in Japanese advertising. Simply stated, both E.T. and Elephant Man confront us with the fear of the out-of-the-ordinary and yet tell us that the fear is misplaced and that the "ugly" unknowns are extremely lovable, like household pets.

Enter Elephant Man and E.T.

Until E.T. came along, American movies treated those from outer space as menacing "aliens," that is, "outsiders" bent on destroying human civilization, just like the Japanese used to feel about foreigners. So there it is—the link with E.T. and Elephant Man;

lovable and "tame" foreigners who were "kept" by Japanese brands helped greatly to alleviate the national persecution complex and to create respect toward the brands that were able to hire them. However, this enjoyed a short phase. With the ascension of Japan to a super economic power status, some of the foreigners appearing on Japanese televison have been reduced to "court jesters."

It is easy enough to expound general principles, but in the world of advertising, these are seldom of practical use. For, E.T. or not, the use of foreign talents does not automatically guarantee the success of a campaign, even if he or she is a super-star. The use of a personality, whether an import or home grown, is an attempt to personalize a brand, or to create memorability with some relevancy to the brand. Thinking back over the years, there are alas very few campaigns with foreigners, considering their numbers, that have made a real impression on the market except the earliest Charles Bronson.

In fact, the use of a personality in Japanese advertising is most often the means to clearly identify a product in a social structure. A product which is purchased for social reasons, therefore, tends to use personalities heavily. For example, 15 years or so ago, when Nissan's Blue Bird was positioned as a car for an up and coming young executive, they used Yuzo Kayama, an actor who portrayed cleancut establishment types destined to middle management. Kayama has now entered his fifties and is no longer used for Blue Bird, but happily appears for many other products. On the other hand, with the greater car ownership since then and the upgrading that has occurred as a result, the positioning for Blue Bird itself underwent such a change that the personality who pushed it was, for a while, Kenji Sawada, the David Bowie of Japan.

In this structured society, where one's status within it is fairly well defined, the use of a personal stereotype is the quickest way to communicate which product one is "expected" to consume. While Western advertisers are often frightened to use a strong personality for fear that their product's destiny may become tied to him, the Japanese have no such qualms and move easily from Kayama to Sawada or from Sammy Davis to David Niven. Note here that it was Suntory White—the lower ranked in the range—rather than Suntory Old or Suntory Reserve for which foreigners were used.

From "Ken and Mary" to "Paul and Paula"

So to finish this exposition of foreigners in Japanese advertising, let me give an example of how a local brand successfully positioned itself with the use of foreigners. In the late 1960s, Nissan produced a commercial for Skyline, tagged "Ken and Mary's Skyline of love." It featured two very clean-cut, presumably American young people. They were not glamorous movie stars but the sort of U.S. "boy and girl next door" types associated with freedom and all that the U.S. car culture signified. It was a hit. "*Ai no* Skyline" (The Skyline of Love) was retained as a catchphrase for the brand long after the departure of Ken and Mary. But after more than ten years, "Ken and Mary" became inappropriate for Skyline with the American car culture losing its attraction. Who should appear in later Skyline commercials but Paul Newman—debonair, masculine, every male's self-image of himself in his fifties. Yes, the fantasy remains so long as foreigners are not part of the community. But with the ownership of a new car no longer the fulfillment of a dream, and with many aspects of the American lifestyle no longer unattainable, the anonymous Ken and Mary ceased to be viable as symbols. Incidentally, a subsequent commercial for the Nissan Langley Car featured—guess who—Paul and Paula, not-too-distant counsins of Ken and Mary, but they could not repeat the success of Ken and Mary.

All Those Foreign-Sounding Brand Names

Why Cedric and Gloria but not Yuzo and Reiko?

ON THE SURFACE, the answer to this question would seem to be simply that the manufcturer wanted to impute a foreign derivation to products, or to attach to them an aura of foreignness. Unfortunately, like the issue of why so many foreigners appear in Japanese advertising, the answer is not quite that simple. Certainly, for some items, this simple explanation holds true, and the brands that readily come to mind are Big John, for blue jeans—a quintessential American product category—and almost all drug names that are not of the herbal veriety. But to the foreigner, it doesn't make sense that comparably priced models from the Nissan stable are called Cedric and Gloria, respectively. Is one supposed to have a masculine positioning and the other a feminine one? Not at all. The gender is just coincidental. Of course, it would be patently ludicrous to have named the cars Yuzo or Reiko—at least that is what we sense intuitively. Is it because the automobiles originally came from the West? No, it is because Yuzo and Reiko are identifiable personal names, while foreign names like Cedric and Gloria remain abstractions.

But that does not entirely explain the fact that Cedric and Gloria are not dissonant to Japanese ears as names for car models. In any case, why do the names have to be foreign? The Japanese know that Nissan, Toyota, and other Japanese makers have a high reputation overseas and, logically, a prestige Japanese car called Kegon (Floral Garland) or Inazuma (Thunderbolt) could easily come into existence. Nevertheless, in the current linguistic environment, I for one would have trouble with these names, but not just because I'm not used to the idea of a purely Japanese name for car models.

The Katakana Phenomenon

Like the foreign talents in Japanese advertising, most Japanese take the phenomena of foreign brand names for granted. However, like foreign talents, the use of the foreign-derived brand names has not always been the same over time. With the talents, the history is a lot shorter; they only started appearing over the last 20 years and it was relatively easy for me to trace their origin. However, the first use of foreign brand names and the reasons for it are much more obscure and cannot be divorced from the evolution of katakana (one of two Japanese phonetic alphabets) as a means to introduce items that were of Western origin and which had no counterparts in Japan at the time. The use of katakana now is not the same as in the earlier periods, and, because of the longer time span for its development, its evolution in conveying foreign words is a lot more complicated than the use of foreigners in advertising.

If any foreign advertiser wishes to understand the internal logic of Japanese advertising, he must at least have a rudimentary knowledge of the unique Japanese system of writing. Of course, this may be more easily said than done for a busy executive. After all, even in the present day, despite efforts to reduce the numbers, the Japanese have to learn at least 2,000 Chinese characters to even be considered "literate." However, learning these will not enable you to read Japanese. As referred to above, the Japanese system also makes simultaneous use of two different sets of syllabic phonetic symbols, each set consisting of just under fifty symbols each.

The written styles of the two syllabaries are quite different and instantly recognizable: *hiragana* are curved, and *katakana* are angular. When the same word is written in *hiragana* or *katakana*, there is simply a different feeling to it which is visually rather than aurally imparted.

In post—World War II writings, *katakana* have been used freely, not only for "foreign-derived words," but also for onomatopoeic words that imitate or suggest what they stand for (e.g., in English, "cuckoo" and "sizzle") and mimesis (word mimicry). In a sentence, *katakana* appear in a supplementary role to the *kanji* (Chinese characters) and *hiragana*, the other form of phonetic writing. However, before the war, *katakana* were used more specifically within ordinances, legal documents, and scholastic treatises, for all sounds not written in *kanji*. I believe that the contemporary usage of *katakana*, by expanding its application, has introduced a sense of dynamism to the modern Japanese language. The fact that until recently, the use of *katakana* was more limited to foreign-derived words tends to confuse us all, including the Japanese, as to its linguistic role. I would contend that the emphasis of *katakana* use has shifted toward an onomatopoeic and the mimetic role, especially in advertising, since coining new words using *katakana* is just so much fun.

There are linguistic chauvinists in any culture who deplore the dilution of their "pure" language. These unfortunates have a rough time in Japan, for hundreds of new words are added to the language each year in *katakana*—not all endure but many do. Some are absolute gems and the two that a foreigner could well acquire in his vocabulary are *nekura* and *neaka,* the former indicating an essentially gloomy and somewhat glum person and the latter, a person with a sunny disposition. It is a combination of *ne* (roots) with either *kurai* (hence, *kura*) meaning gloomy and *akarui* (hence, *aka*) meaning bright, cheerful. Everybody is running around classifying their friends and colleagues in either of these two terms. Of course, since most would prefer to be called *neaka* (a cheerful and positive person), let us hope that this has a brightening effect on social attitudes. The birth of *neaka* and *nekura* is just one out of many examples of ingenious combination of syllables in *katakana* that add a fresh dimension to communication.

The Japanese themselves love to review the new words that come into being, usually during the New Year period, when they look back over the previous year. One hilarious example of a word that was in the Japanese lexicon in the early 1980s is *mantoru.* When I first saw it in *katakana,* I did not know what it meant and a surprised young Japanese colleague had to explain to me that it signified a "call girl trade operated from a private apartment." You see, when prostitution became illegal, even in the renowned establishments such as graced Yoshiwara, it shifted into the seedier premises of the Turkish bath houses. Now Turkey in Japanese is *Toruko,* so the Turkish bath in Japanese was once known as *Toruko buro.* I must add that due to pressure from the government of Turkey, such an establishment is no longer known as a *toruko* but as *sōpurando* (Soap Land). All foreign residents in Japan know that if an apartment is of a certain class, it is a "mansion." So, apartment-operated prostitution is *mantoru* and a hotel operated one is *hotetoru*. Get it? A further linguistic development is that super luxury apartments are now called *okushons* because the *man* part of "mansion" in Japanese has the same sound as the number "ten thousand," so instead of *man*, the larger *oku*, which is "a hundred million" in Japanese, is used as the prefix.

Katakana's *Clarifying Role in Communication*

Nobody thinks of these words as "foreign," and to talk of them as of foreign origin misses the point. To illustrate the importance of onomatopoeia and the contribution of *katakana* in this context, we should consider the spate of corporate name changes that have hit Japan as a result of the so-called CI (or corporate identity) boom. In 1983, fifteen top companies registered on the Tokyo Stock Exchange changed their corporate names, an increase over the twelve that did so in 1982. Kyoto Ceramics became Kyocera, and Tokyo Shibaura Denki officially became Toshiba, an abbreviation of its company name that had become a well-known brand name. Toshiba, interestingly, retains its identity in *kanji* (Chinese characters) while Kyocera is part *kanji* and part *katakana*. Keihin Sokō (the latter word meaning warehouse) changed its name to Keijin because warehousing now accounts for less than one-fifth of its business. However, for Keihin, Toshiba's way of simply retaining the two initial *kanji* was not possible because Keihin is a district that encompasses Tokyo and Yokohama—so their company name, Keihin, was simply rendered into *katakana*. By doing so, the name has a certain abstraction and, although pronounced exactly the same as the district, it can no longer be confused with it.

So, one effective use of *katakana* is in changing a word which has a specific meaning into an abstraction—like International Business Machines becoming IBM. It reduces the element of confusion in communication, so it is not surprising that the process of using *katakana* is most often associated with foreign words, because they are, by definition, the least clear in meaning. It made obvious sense when Riken Kōgaku Kōgyō (all in *kanji*) became Ricoh in the 1960s—Ricoh in *katakana* is comprised of the first syllables of each of the two words which in turn comprise the original company name, and it was perhaps fortuitous that the new name had a foreign ring. The company may, of course, have welcomed this foreignness because of its Western-technology-based product range and for its export drive. But probably, more importantly, it was an attempt to create a modern image, and here we reach the crux of the matter. For, in the past, modernization and Westernization was indistinguishable, although the tendency of equating the two is rapidly diminishing.

Everybody Can Pronounce Katakana, *Not Everybody,* Kanji

Sometimes, there is an even simpler reason for using a *katakana* brand name. As stated earlier, there are at least 2,000 *kanji* that Japanese have to learn and it is true that almost all Japanese have mastered them. *Kanji* is a visual means of communication and it is not always possible for one to be able to pronounce their various combinations even if one actually knows the individual characters. Yamato Unyu (transportation) changed the Yamato part to *katakana* because in *kan-ji* it could also be read as Daiwa. Asahi Bīru (Beer) has changed *bīru* in all its letter heads and advertising material from *kanji* to *katakana*. It was claimed that the less "educated" modern generation sometimes pronounced the *kanji* as *mugishu* (barley saké). In any event, the *katakana* is undeniably more modern in feeling and so two purposes were served. Suntory, the famed manufacturer of alcoholic beverages, was called Kotobukiya until the 1960s. Apart from being extremely old fashioned in feeling—that of a vintage liquor store—this name too would be unpronounceable to quite a few if given in the Chinese characters. Although the importance of visual elements in Japanese advertising communication is acknowledged, it is still preferable to have a pronounceable name.

When did It Start?

To delve into the origin of *katakana* or foreign sounding brand names, I went to Dentsu's *History of the Development of Advertising in Japan (Nihon Kokoku Hattatsushi,* ed. Yoshimi Uchikawa, 2 vols.). Unfortunately, this superb publication is not available in English, but according to it, the first example appeared in the 1860s, in the form of a *hikifuda,* which is the ancestor of the modern *chirashi*—a flyer. This was not surprising because it was in the early Meiji era—or mid-nineteenth century—in which Western products first started to make their appearances in urban Tokyo. The flyer was for a drug called *Kindoru-san* with the first part in *katakana* and the *san* in *kanji* (which is not to be confused with the Japanese personal honorific). To totally confuse most of my Western readers, *san,* the personal honorific, is written in *hiragana,* the other phonetic form of writing,

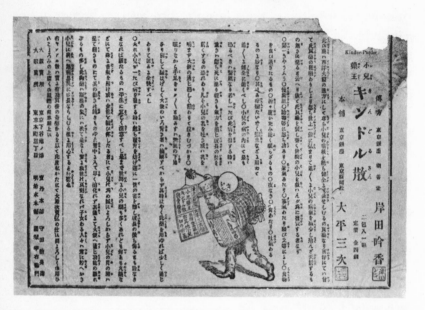

The flyer for *Kindoru-san* with the heading in *katakana* and *kanji*.

but it was the Chinese character, *san,* that was used in this case, indicating that the drug was in powdered form. Western medicine was only just beginning to be popularly introduced and thus the product name suggested a curious mixture of a Western laboratory-produced item with a traditional herbal ingredient. In fact, almost as if to illustrate this schizophrenic positioning, the flyer showed a bearded character in a bowler hat carrying a traditionally kimono-clad child on his back. There were no features on the child's face but instead the *katakana* for *Kindoru.* The copy was on an almost vintage herbal platform.

Katakana *Names Signify Modernism*

I was fascinated that this was the first example that I could find of a *katakana* brand name, because all Western-type drugs have ever since followed this custom of *katakana* brand names while pure herbal remedies have retained their *kanji* identities. Assuming it was permitted by the Ministry of Health, the simple expedience of giving the same drug a *katakana* and *kanji* name will enable the manufacturer to position the drug in two distinct consumer segments, in one fell swoop, without going to the bother of developing separate formulae. A recent twist is that some herbal remedies have appeared in *katakana,* and this seeming contradiction can be explained by the very early advertising of *Kindoru-san,* namely that the product combines the best of two worlds for those who would like to have the security of tradition but some of the adventures of modernism. Is this not characteristic of the Japanese culture?

カタカナ	かたかな	片仮名
"Katakana" in *katakana*	"Katakana" in *hiragana*	"Katakana" in *kanji*

The Place of Champions in Japan

The Yomiuri Giants

JUST AS A LOT OF people tell me the Japanese are becoming Westernized, a lot of people tell me the Japanese youths are rapidly changing in their tastes. This is true enough in their experimentation with new things, so visible everywhere we go. It would be a troubled world indeed if the youths were not restless and active in their search for new values. One thing hasn't changed in Japan, though, and it is the adoration given to the Yomiuri Giants by young and old throughout the country. Admittedly, this is not quite as strong in the Western regions, as the Yomiuri Giants are ostensibly a Tokyo team. However, it is estimated that if we include any baseball fans who are "involved" in the Giants, that would cover the great majority of the adult Japanese population. That is to say, you may not be cheering for them, but by their being the team you would love to see lose, you are, in fact, strongly "involved" in their fate, even if negatively.

This can be demonstrated quite simply by the TV audience ratings

for games in which the Giants don't play—they are abysmal. These
nongames are only occasionally shown during peak viewing time,
but mostly by NHK, the Japanese equivalent of BBC, not because
they feel they have an obligation to serve minority tastes but mainly
because they don't have to worry about getting a sponsor for the
time slot when the Giants are playing on another channel. The Seibu
Lions, however, more often the champs in recent years—but playing
in the neglected Pacific League—have not been able to generate
anything like the enthusiasm that surronds the mystique of the
Giants, and yet the Seibu promotional machine is a formidable one,
as it has shown by its ability to tap the youth market in other areas.

In the 1984 season, neither the Lions nor the Giants did well, with
the former plunging to the second last position in its league.
Whatever following the Lions had virtually evaporated that year.
However, even if the Giants have not a chance in a million of winning the pennant in any given year, their following and audience
ratings on TV remain unaffected, a situation that is unheard of for
other teams. In fact a game with the Giants that was merely to fill
out the season's commitment, and which had no bearing on the pennant, drew a larger crowd than the one that was to decide the
league's winner. But by winning the 1986, 1987 and 1988 pennants
to become the Japan champions for three successive years, the Lions
are on the rise with new, young star players but still have a long way
to go to catch the Giants in ratings.

Remaining in the Spotlight—No Matter What

There was a time when the Giants finished at the bottom of their
league during the first year of the management of the now retired,

all-time hero, third baseman Shigeo Nagashima—who had, as a player, been dubbed by his fans "Mr. Giants." Everybody went along to watch the Giants get a clobbering and to bemoan the poor state of the world that had allowed this sad thing to happen. Yet despite their poor showing that year, the Giants' players dominated—at least in numbers—the Central League's line-up for the the All Star Games. (Unlike the United States, which has only one of these games in a season, Japan has three.)

Not surprisingly, since they were represented by players from the team that had the poorest performance record, the Central team was soundly defeated by the Pacific team in the first two games. In fact, the Pacific teams have had a handy lead over the Central teams for the All Star Games over the years, but attendance at their games is only a fraction of that for the Central teams, for whom members of the Giants play. But all that aside, the third game was won by the Central team with the help of Egawa, the Giants' pitcher who retired in 1987 (and one you either loved or hated), who performed outstandingly with 8 strike-outs in a row. The next day, Egawa's pitching was all that baseball fans talked about—the fact that the Pacific League won the series was all but forgotten. The performance by other Pacific League players who contributed to the winning of the series paled in comparison with the performance of this one Giants player. In his first game after the All Stars, Egawa got knocked out, again providing the one and only topic of conversation in baseball the next day.

Newsstand sales of sports dailies increase if some dramatic headline can be given to something related to the Giants. Among sports personalities, Giants players dominate TV commercials. And so on and so on. Perhaps at their peak those "damned Yankees" had it like this—and that's a long time ago and they were a spectacular team anyway. When I first returned to Japan—for this is the country of my birth—I was considerably irked by all this. I was irritated that the only way to get to know players of other teams was when they played against the Giants. I was tired of the same Giants team members continuously occupying my TV screen. And then a subtle change in me took place that indeed indicated that I had become "Japanized." If I had had a head office, they would surely be saying, "Fields has been out there too long. He is becoming one of them, . . . losing perspective, . . . time for a change." The realization came with a shock when I heard myself saying to a taxi driver—what else is there to talk about when he has the ball game on his car radio—that this year's Japan Series is not going to be too much fun because the Giants would probably not be playing. It was an Osaka cabby but he was not offended—he agreed wholeheartedly!

Then I remembered when I went to Tokorozawa, the Seibu Lion's home ground; the only way of getting there is to take a Seibu train, traveling for some 40 minutes out of central Tokyo. Anybody who knows me well would have been astonished because I hate crowds and go to great lengths to avoid them. (You may ask, how do you do it in Tokyo?"—but this is one secret I am not going to divulge.) Still, I did go and exulted in the Lions' victory over the Giants. I won't go to Korakuen, the Giants' home ground, because I get intimidated by the overwhelming majority of Giants supporters and the astonishingly well-trained and disciplined Giants' "private" cheering squad. (It is, however, necessary to go at least once as an educational experience if you are a student of Japanese culture.) The point is that, I thought I went because I was a Lions fan, but now I know better—I went because there was a possibility of my seeing the Lions beat the Giants, and that would have been exciting. Come to think of it, when the Lions became the champions the previous year,

on TV because they were only beating the Chūnichi
̄ver occurred to me then to travel out to Tokorozawa
to see that series.

Not Just a Ball Club

The leading Japanese monthly magazine, *Bungei Shunjū,* ran a feature
in its June 1984 issue with the title, "The Japanese and the Giants."
The subheading was "With the demise of the Giants will come the
demise of Japan." I would not be surprised if this issue of *Bungei
Shunjū* attained record sales. It is a serious magazine and the
"demise" bit was said only half in jest. The writer, Takashi Iwasaki,
concluded his article thus:

> One has to win, no matter what. So long as there is a winning
> streak, that organization is stable and safe. If you win, you are the
> official army. If you lose, everything goes to pot. What makes one
> suppress the 'individual' and dedicate to the 'whole' when the
> group knows that it is going to be defeated? The Japanese, and
> Japan as a country in its basic characteristics, carries within it the
> 'weakness' that it is ordained to keep on winning, no matter
> what. The Giants suffer from the same ordination. And such a
> team is now continuing to lose, so what is the world coming to?
> Are both the world and Japan changing?

The equation of the Giants and Japan, or the idea that the Giants
symbolize the "natural" state of Japan, is interesting. But it does
make sense to me as a marketer, looking with some detachment from

the outside. So let us examine the proposition that the Giants symbolize the Japanese market.

Obligations that Come with Status

First, there is respect for the status and the obligation imposed upon leaders to discharge their duties with dignity. In sumo, the *yokozuna*—the grand champion—is not supposed to lose—at least not too often. To him, there is not the luxury afforded others of the *kachikoshi* (8 wins and 7 losses) keeping him in his place. If there is the danger that he may lose more than he wins, or even if he may only just squeak through, he usually is diagnosed as suffering from some obscure ailment and retires from the rest of the tournament to recuperate. If the *yokozuna* cannot maintain a minimum of 10 wins out of 15 bouts in too many consecutive tournaments, he retires altogether, mostly—but not always—to become the head of his own stable. To "play the game like a *yokozuna*" [*Yokozuna sumo o toru*] is an expression that is often used when the manner of winning is appropriate to the dignity of a grand champion.

In the fall tournament of 1987, Onokuni, performing for the first time as a member of this exalted rank, lost his first three consecutive matches. He bravely stayed on to squeak through with an 8-7 record of wins and losses. It was pointed out by some critics that this was the worst record of any *yokozuna* in modern sumo history, and there was great concern. But at the end of the year, the sumo world would be stunned by the behavior of another relatively newly elevated champion, an event discussed later in this chapter in another context "The Group's Still the Thing."

Corporations as Community Leaders

Certain corporations and brands are *yokozunas* of their category and they are expected to behave as such, and they do, indeed, take their obligations seriously.

In 1984 JAL was faced with a horrendous situation when a mentally disturbed pilot crashed his plane into Tokyo Bay, just off the Haneda runway, killing and seriously injuring many passengers. It was not just a case of legal liability. The airline's president personally visited every affected family and prostrated himself. A senior executive was assigned to each family to look after their needs. In startling contrast to the tragic Korean Airlines dispute, not one family sued JAL at the beginning and most settled out of court. However, in 1985 a JAL jumbo crashed into a mountainside near Tokyo, killing all but three out of the 524 passengers and crew aboard and creating a new world record in the number of fatalities in a single aircraft crash. Causes and culpability were argued, but the magnitude of the disaster and the succession of major incidents shook the airline's standing in the community, spawning a host of litigations—a very *un*-Japanese situation, indeed.

These upheavals within a Japanese corporation are, as in the West, accompanied by a change in management. However, when a major corporation tarnishes its image by behavior not befitting its social status—even if the circumstances are beyond the control of the current management—it may have to suffer the consequences of past managerial misdemeanor, even though the offending managers may already have been replaced. The blame cannot be laid upon an individual manager, no matter how senior, for the *corporation* is the *yokozuna,* and not the individual. The road to recovery can be very arduous and long, as was the case with a food company struck with disaster a long time ago, and it appears to be so in the fairly more recent case of a major retailer.

The venerable Mitsukoshi department store was not only the oldest in Japan but also the largest for a long time. However, it was involved in a Middle Eastern antique scandal and was blamed for having made its space available to a couple of dealers who turned out to be shady operators. This was the last straw that brought down the rule of an autocratic and unpopular president of the department store, one who also proved to be tainted in his personal dealings as well.

In what amounted to a coup-d'état, the president was fired at a board meeting—something that was both unprecedented and unheard of in the annals of Japanese corporate history. It is more common for upper-level executives not to be fired but to be made "advisors" of the company.

The errant president was not only fired, he was also sued, and a completely new management—made up of those who had been either at loggerheads with him or side-lined—was brought in. Having cleaned house, one would have expected that the store would have been able to return to business as usual, but this was not the case. Mitsukoshi suffered a severe decline in sales and remained in the doldrums for several years. It seems that the community was punishing the store for not living up to its obligations as a *yokozuna* in the retailing world: the pressure to behave properly was exerted socially rather than legally.

The Boys of Summer and a New Corporate Identity

In my recent sojourn in Europe, I was struck by the steady progress in the global dissemination of information. Of course, U.S. news has been immediately available for some time but while I did not get a Japanese paper with my breakfast, I read about the discomforts of a Japanese minister in parliament concerning insider trading, a gangland murder and much on the foibles of the Japanese consumer.

When it comes to business news, there are no borders and takeover battles are now digested every morning along with corn-flakes or miso soup. Still, an item I did not expect in my morning paper in London concerned the Braves baseball team being sold by the Hankyu Corp. to Orient Leasing Co.

Of course, mergers and acquisitions have occurred in Japan too, but the Japanese approach has been very different and they tend to see the activities going on in the United States and Europe as peculiarly Western aberrations. Mergers in Japan have tended to be engineered by the banks who bail out an ailing operation, often at the instigation of a government ministry — e.g., C. Itoh & Co.'s absorption of Ataka & Co. — or by agreement between the companies to gain a larger market share — e.g., Nippon Steel Corp.

The merger of two banks, the Dai-Ichi Bank and Nippon Kangyo Bank, which made it number one in size, involved me as a customer. My company has an account with Dai-Ichi Kangyo Bank and it was necessary for me one day to drop into my branch, close to the office. However, to my puzzlement, I found myself in the wrong branch — my branch was the next one down, with only a small street in be-tween! At the time of the merger, one of them was Dai-Ichi and one was Kangyo, so when they both became Dai-Ichi Kangyo, one became the Shimbashi branch and the other the Hibiya branch and they proceeded to compete vigorously for business in close proximity to each other. My experience is 15 years old but the two branches are still there. In the Western context, the main benefit of such a merger would have been the elimination of redundancies, so one of them would have been closed. With such fundamental differences in business philosophies, it is no wonder that Japanese companies prefer going the 100 percent route rather than a joint venture when they move overseas.

On the return trip to Tokyo, I was able to catch up with the full story of the change of ownership of the Braves. It was called, *miuri* — the usual term for sales of one company to another — which translates as "selling of bodies." There was an outpouring of emotion by fans and players of this once proud team (they were champions several times in the past). When the Brooklyn Dodgers moved to Los Angeles, there was also an emotional response driven by the geographical identification of the team, as all American teams are local heroes. However, this is not the case in Japan, where 10 out of the 12 teams are in either the Tokyo or Osaka areas. The Braves will stay in Osaka, so in the American context, the fans should not be upset.

The difference between American and Japanese professional baseball teams is that, with the former, a team is identified with an area. But in Japan, with the exception of the Hiroshima Carp, a team closely identified with the city, Japanese teams carry the owner's corporate name, e.g., the current champion team Seibu Lions' prefix is that of a railway and hotel group. The Levi's Athletics?! The fans and the players of the Dodgers in the U.S. were greatly disturbed because of the geographic shift, but the Braves' fans in Japan resisted the change in corporate identity.

Thus, the new owner took great pains to assure continuity in all aspects — team composition, management and above all, in the team tradition. Despite this, the miffed manager — he was not let in on the decision — hinted at his departure and declared his great attach-

‍ the previous identity. The fact that the team was not necessarily treated well under the old management seems to have been forgotten. Two star players, in the twilight of their careers (one holds the world record for bases stolen) announced their retirement; due anyway, but the opportunity to express their sadness at the change in corporate identity was not missed.

Corporate identity is only a fairly recent entry in the Western marketing mix, associated too often just with the company name, logo, or facades of outlets. In the consumer goods area, companies are bought because of their brands and not because of their corporate culture. In Japan, corporate identity is just as strong an element — sometimes stronger — as brand identity. Consumers, who tend to be salaried workers themselves, reason that a company with a cavalier attitude toward its employees is likely to be contemptuous of its customers. It is not surprising that CI (Corporate Identity) has become a buzz word in Japanese marketing and that the now legendary Asahi Super Dry Beer resulted from a very intensive CI program instituted by the new president which, in turn, produced a climate conducive to product innovation. Here, you can lose or gain market share through your corporate identity and that is why a change in ownership is not taken lightly.

The Desire for Stable Markets

Also, in the above, we can see the desire for stability—the winner to be always the winner—which affects so much of Japanese business relationships. The Japanese have a word, *katō kyōsō* ("excessive competition") which is trotted out every time some newcomer upsets the balance between brands in the market place, especially so when the newcomer happens to be foreign. The entry of Procter & Gamble was particularly unpopular, as they made no bones about aiming to be brand leader. The marketing cliché in Japan is that major product categories are dominated by 1 to 4 brands and their shares tend to be relatively stable over their total range (e.g., Lion and Sunstar in the dentifrice market; Suntory and Nikka in whisky; Shiseido and Kanebo in cosmetics; Toyota and Nissan in cars; Honda and Yamaha in bikes; etc.). It was Kao and Lion that had to meet the challenge of a Western "usurper," Procter & Gamble, and tempers were frayed in the early periods.

Order or chaos? If it was as simple as that, the choice would be obvious. We know that the great attraction of living in Japan is in its orderliness. We can walk the clean streets of Tokyo in the early hours without fear of molestation and the trains run impeccably, on time. These are aspects that I sorely miss when out of Japan. Therefore rightly, order is a valued Japanese societal quality and there are many guardians of it; the Japanese have continuously voted for order if there was only a faint chance that the alternative would upset some established harmony.

When applied to situations where international pressures are not present, it seems to be the first option. This was in evidence in July 1977 when the Japanese Fair Trades Commission (FTC) allowed the formation of a cartel which would set a consistent standard for the transfer of the proposed consumption tax on to the retail price. The Japanese FTC said that cartels would only be allowed among medium to small enterprises who have to register the fact with them. Clearly, collusion among the marketers, no matter what size, deprives the consumers of the benefit of competition and the trade-off is the maintenance of orderliness in the market.

In an extraordinary statement to the press, Mr. Setsuo Umezawa, the head of the FTC, asked the consumers to be watchful of those who took advantage of the situation and raised prices. "It would be desirable for consumers and the administration to work together toward the control of illegal acts," he said. My Japanese colleagues didn't seem to be particularly surprised with the statement but I found it remarkable, coming from a body who is supposed to be a watchdog of consumer interests. Anyway, as a consumer, I'm not sure how I can gather facts that prove illegality, even if I had the time.

"Group Maternalism" versus "Individualism"

Easily shooting off my mouth like that, I never dreamed that I would personally face the Japanese FTC, but it happened in November 1988. I was one of nine who testified on the pros and cons of a possible change. Bowing to American pressure, it was proposed that premium offers for chocolates could be brought into line with other products. If the Americans had their way, no such restrictions would be placed on any products in Japan but at least this was a start.

Testimonies were given by three each from consumer groups and academia, an Agricultural Ministry official, a retail store manager and yours truly. The three female representatives of the consumer groups, who spoke first, were unanimously against the proposed amendment, especially as "easily tempted" children were buyers of chocolates. Given their own way, they indicated they would make conditions stricter rather than easier. Most of the others gave qualified support to the relaxation of the rules; industry only grudgingly, sacrificing to the national interest of relieving the trade friction. I had entered a tiger's den because I was the only one to give unqualified support. Many of the testimonies left the impression that the Americans were trying to force their own values on another society.

Commenting on the respective stances on "fair trade," I often use the example of sumo versus boxing. In sumo, there is no discrimination between the combatants, by size; currently a popular combat is between a Hawaiian born behemoth, Konishiki, against a, for sumo, relatively dimunitive scrapper called Terao, who only weighs about half of the former. On paper, the probability of winning is heavily weighted toward the Hawaiian. The way the Japanese see it, in real life, those without natural advantages must compensate for it by acquiring special skills. In boxing, while Sugar Ray Leonard has acomplished the feat of capturing titles in five divisions, nevertheless, lightweights don't fight heavyweights because they would be murdered. The sumo rule as applied to business provides a natural advantage to the established and the large, against which the newcomer — read foreign enterprises — and the small must cope. The American attitude is that "fairness" means extending "equal opportunity," so an arena in which one side does not have a pronounced advantage should be granted.

When the game rules differ so much, there is bound to be a squabble. The Americans contend that, unlike the Japanese distribution system which is weighted heavily toward the established and the large, premiums and coupons provide one of the few arenas in the Japanese market place where the battle can be fought on equal terms. Well, not quite, since yuou still have to have the money. A point was made by one of the consumer representatives who said that if the law were revised, small businesses would be at a disadvantage. It is such compassion for the less efficient that keeps the prices so high for her constituents. Anyway, she has her facts wrong because premiums are most often given out by the smaller confectionery manufacturers to compensate for their lack of clout. There is no reason for the big ones to resort to such methods given their secure market shares.

The Japanese consumer representatives appeared weak on facts because they seemed to have the notion that competition led to a rise in prices. Promotional costs are passed on to the consumer, they reasoned, but the evidence is that consumers are poorly placed in societies that restrict promotional activities. After all, the final arbiter of the promotion's efficacy is the consumer.

Explaining the basic differences in attitudes on this issue alas sounds like pop sociology. First, "Group maternalism" — I prefer the "m" to the "p" because of the sex of the consumer representatives — could be imputed to the Japanese and "individualism" to the Americans. The Japanese consumer representatives had the maternal concern that their constituents would be "duped" into acquiring things that they didn't need through such devices as premiums. It was the duty of the wise in society to protect and guide others. A typical American reaction would be that it is nobody's business whether an individual decides to buy something based on a premium offer. Why shouldn't a child make the decision to buy a combination of candy and something else from his or her own pocket money? If any guidance is to be offered, it should more likely come from the parent or the teacher, not from a third party.

The second difference, again phrased in pop sociology, would be "social harmony" versus "consumer sovereignty." In Japan, there is sympathy for victims of "excessive" competition who are not the consumers but the producers. Consumers, it is agreed, generally benefit from a price war, except when safety is involved. One industry representative stated that price competition with imports was "unfair" because the Japanese manufacturers were compelled to buy expensive local base materials. A fair comment. Like their overseas competitors, they should have access to the cheapest source, even if that meant not buying from a Japanese supplier. In the official American stance, if certain manufacturers get hurt because of competition, so be it; this is the normal mechanism for structural adjustment. Of course, the move toward protectionism contradicts this.

But as for the alien concept of "consumer sovereignty," are the Japanese consumers so naive that they will keep buying an inferior product just because premiums are given with it? Not according to my research. Without repurchase, the cost of enticing the consumer to try at a discount cannot be recouped and that means making sure that the product provides continued satisfaction. If consumers keep buying a product of reduced quality because of a continued premium offer — like they swap cards — that is because a trade-off is made between getting one product only and a combination of appeals. Are they incapable of making that decision themselves? Japanese consumer representatives should be reminded that, in another context, they repeatedly proclaim that their constituents are the most fastidious and wisest in the world. They cannot have it both ways.

The Importance of Spotting a Market Gap and Acting Quickly

The year 1987 marked a turning point in the Japanese market and seemed to challenge many long-cherished clichés. Until 1987, I could confidently say that great marketing successes in Japan tended to be the result of a creation of a genre rather than dramatic encroachment on the established brands. One created the genre, then one went on to become the "winner." In the early days, Ajinomoto was such a case, and Coca Cola and Nestlé became postwar winners by preempting their respective categories. There are, of course, exceptions, but the upsetting of the incumbent and disturbing of the market equilibrium by a brash newcomer, which is very much a part of the marketing scene in the U.S.—Tylenol's coming from nowhere to become the number one analgesic is a remarkable story but one that has been repeated—seems to occur less frequently here.

In my observation over the last twenty years, new brand successes still tend to come from established stables. Of course, established marketers have an advantage in the United States too, and new stables emerge in Japan as well, but it seems to take much longer, on the average, for them to crack the market in a big way than in the United States. This is because just winning the Japan Series two or three times doesn't make the Seibu Lions the equivalent of the Giants.

This leads to the observation that speed of entry is all important before the market stabilizes. It is perhaps best to enter into a relatively underdeveloped category or, better still, create a new one and establish your *yokozuna* status there. This may be why so much effort is placed by Japanese manufacturers on the importing of product ideas as quickly as possible from overseas and the establishment of a brand franchise. Alas, as a researcher over the years, I have often had to watch Western clients go through the standard process of test marketing, only to see their competitors whip in with the same product concept earlier than them and preempt the market. There are few secrets that can be kept in the tightly knit community that is Japan and you are open game if you choose to display yourself to all and sundry in a test market. If only some of the pretest market laboratory techniques, which have become so developed and are available in Japan now, had been applied earlier, who knows, there would now be more Western brands with *yokozuna* status!

The Whole is Greater than the Parts: The Umbrella Franchise

The Yomiuri Giants embodied yet another Japanese cliché, one which states that the whole is greater than the parts. Nagashima—the very man dubbed "Mr. Giants" in his heyday—is no longer associated with the Giants. After dismissal as their manager, he has staunchly refused to answer the wooings of other teams. And yet he no longer partakes of the magic of being a Giant.

Tatsuro Hirooka—the manager of the Lions who first triumphed over the Giants in 1983 and an ex-Giant himself—continuously refers to the Giants as the one team worth defeating. The fact that he was tossed out of the Giants team during his pro-ball days adds a certain grandeur to this stance.

Masaaki Mori, his successor, who has done even better by defeating the Giants in both the 1986 and 1987 seasons—the Giants were not even in the running in 1988—maintains the same tradition of unceasingly referring to the Giants as his worthy foe. He, too, is an ex-Giant.

Isao Harimoto, a superstar who played for the Toei Flyers, publicly stated, after joining the Giants in the twilight years of his playing career, that he now realized what it meant to suppress one's individual glory and sacrifice one's self for the sake of the team. Coming from Harimoto, I am inclined to take this with a few grains of salt, but such an attitude is certainly admired by the community.

Now you can see the advantage of developing a brand franchise under a single umbrella. Examples in the retail world come extremely easily to mind—Suntory, Toyota, Shiseido, Kao, Lion, etc.—1987 was a bad year for both Suntory and Shiseido and 1988 for Lion. Are the times changing?

Now for "Internationalization"

The Giants epitomize the problems that Western concerns encounter when attempting to enter the Japanese scene: namely, stability under a few designated *local* authorities.

In the 1960s, the Giants were proud of the fact that they were the top dog without the help of any foreign players. It is acknowledged now that no team—and the Giants are no exception—can hope to win the pennant without some good foreign players among their ranks. In fact, the presence of such players is usually the difference that tips the balance.

The Japanese apply the term *suketto* (which means something like "hired gun" among other things) to all foreign players imported to boost the level of the team. But it also applies to Japanese transplants, too, although not as strongly. Kurosawa's great film *The Seven Samurai* was on the theme of *suketto,* and dealt with how these rescuers who had saved the peasants from a marauding band of bandits were discarded after they had served their purpose. Robert Whiting's *The Chrysanthemum and the Bat* takes an entertaining look at Japanese culture through the eyes of the foreign *suketto* players.

There have been a few outstanding examples of successful domestic transplants; for example, Harimoto, who was an excellent batter, and Kaneda, who is an all-time pitching great, joined the Giants late in their careers. But regardless of whether or not they are foreign or Japanese—Davy Johnson, manager of the New York Mets was one of the former—transplants have, by and large, proved to be unsuccessful or short lived, and one suspects that there may be some invisible pressure exerted upon them as "outsiders." There have of late been a few outstanding survivors who adopted to the ways of their teams; a parallel can be drawn with the struggle of foreign businesses with the distribution networks.

The Year of the Drop-Outs

In the summer of 1985, the topic in the taxi from Osaka airport to the hotel turned inevitably to the surprising emergence of the Hanshin Tigers as the leader in Japanese baseball's Central League. "Aren't the Tigers terrific!" "Nah, they will never make it," was the response. "You see, they have this *mano rōdo* coming up." This literally translates as the "road of misfortune," and refers to their traveling tours, which take place because their home ground, Koshien, has to be given up to the biannual high-school baseball frenzy, causing the team to go on the road during the steaming month of August. Thus, for this local Osaka team, the dice was loaded.

All comments—expert or otherwise—were pessimistic about the Tigers' possible triumph. They were a perennial runner-up and their failure some ten years ago still haunted the ardent Hanshin fans. Then, as now, there were stars on the team and all they had to do was to win one game out of the final three to take the pennant. Well, they didn't, and they were defeated by the Yomiuri Giants who went on to take the Japan Series. Commentators had a whale of a time saying that this final show of weakness was inherent in the character of the team, which was full of individual stars but had little team spirit.

The Giants, considered a triumph of managerial efficiency and the subjugation of the individual to the team, had not been champs for several years, but, as discussed above, they remained the public favorite. As noted earlier, the rise of the maverick Hanshin Tigers in 1985 and Seibu Lions subsequently and the consequent threat to the Giants was seen by many as a national crisis.

I missed the Tigers' final triumph despite a valued invitation ticket because I was in the States watching the Royals on TV, as they turned the tables on the Cardinals. I returned to Japan, wisely skipping the Narita-to-Tokyo route, and climbed my weary body into an Osaka taxi. "I hear the Tigers were spectacular." "Well," he said, "it was a day for drop-outs." That was a profound statement. There was something in the event that heralded to some the entry of a new era, when strict management control and establishment strength could be upset by a bunch of individuals.

Then I thought of *shōchū,* the lowly alcoholic drink that played havoc with the performances of corporate giants like Suntory: Consumer revolt against the establishment, in turn, heralding the individualization of the market? "I guess this is a new era in baseball," I said to my taxi driving friend, "Nah," he said, "It's a fluke. They'll never make it next year."

In 1986, the Tigers again dropped out, and in 1987, they not only occupied the last place in the league but even broke all records for poor performance. In 1987, *shōchū,* too, suffered a decline in sales.

But Incumbents — and Together, Japanese Marketing Myths — Can Tumble

But towards mid 1988, some started to say that "The marketing megatrend in Japan is the demise of the megabrand." It may be premature to propose that as a new Japanese marketing maxim, since it can be countered by citing the still totally unassailable positions some brands occupy in the market.

Nevertheless, enough evidence is at hand to suggest that this comfortable environment for the majors is fast disappearing. The advent of the "Super Dry" beer, triggered by the Asahi Beer Company, has created a furor in the Japanese marketing community. The turn-around engineered by a perennial number three brewer who, with a steadily eroding position, doubled market·share in less than two years, catching up with number two, would have been remarkable in any country. The significance is that it was achieved not just in any market but in Japan. Giving heart to consumer marketers, it has proven that with a good product concept, a concept-matching product and a dynamic campaign, even a giant market leader can be shaken. Kirin commanded a share close to 60% in 1986 and saw it dwindle to almost 50% with the advent of Super Dry. For the first time in 13 years, Kirin registered a significant decline; for the half year ending June 1988, sales were down by 2.8% over the year before and profits by 17.7%. In contrast, for the same period, Asahi's sales were up by a whopping 53.8% and profit by 40.7%.

In 1982, I discussed the hierarchical nature of brand positioning among alcoholic beverages, particularly in whiskey, in my book, *From Bonsai to Levi's*. I could not have predicted then that Asahi would emerge among the top 30 most-favored firms for employment listed by college seniors, and·that Suntory, then the number three in preference, would not even appear in the list five years later.

Even for automobiles, Japan is beginning to resemble Detroit — at least in the battle for brand share. The high-flying Ford and the stagnant General Motors have been a favorite recent topic for American business journalists. True, Toyota dominates the nation's total passenger car registration with a share of 40%, more than double that of the second-ranking Nissan. However, since early 1988, an unusual seesaw battle has developed in the lucrative and fastest-growing segment of larger-sized passenger cars. Admittedly, it accounted for only about 3% of all passenger car registrations in 1987. But with the introduction of Nissan's Cima, Toyota Crown's top position is now threatened, even if temporarily. Again, it is an important distinction that Cima as a model, rather than Nissan as a company, is giving the Crown a run.

At the other end of the scale, in the mini-car category, a similar battle is raging between the two leaders, Suzuki and Daihatsu. Suzuki, a pioneer in the market for light vans, established a superior distribution network early. However, it's now a neck-and-neck position with Daihatsu; the latter's rise is accredited to targeting young women (females account for 60% of the usership of mini-cars, but the proportion is 70% for Daihatsu's Mirror). It's a case of style, with name and image overcoming a distribution handicap.

The prime example of maintaining market dominance through control of distribution is the tobacco industry. All deliverers to outlets were subsidiaries of the former governmental monopoly, now privatized. The industry thought it could "give a certain proportion" to foreign brands to alleviate trade tension, but the consumer has played havoc with their expectations. Foreign brands grabbed 10% of the market in 1987, up from 4% in 1986; some say it will reach 15% by the end of 1988. In trendsetting areas, foreign cigarettes share could easily be double of the national average. To those — in both the United States and Japan — who maintain that Japanese consumers place priority on local producers, this must come as quite a shock.

To dispel another Japanese myth held by many overseas that Japan is the home of cartels and cozy market share arrangements, a fierce contest is stewing in laptop computers, facsimiles and word processors. The fight is being waged over factors such as size and weight versus functions, software, compatibility, etc.; these factors, rather than distribution strength, or even to some extent corporate image, will determine the winner. Being first in the market is no longer a permanent guarantee for success, as evidenced in both the facsimile and word processor categories. For the former, Ricoh has caught up with the long-time leader Matsushita and for the latter, in the number of units produced, Sharp has overtaken Toshiba. In many respects, the Japanese market is much the same animal I wrote about in 1982; but the rigid infrastructure is fast crumbling.

The Group's Still the Thing

Two Japanese stars shook the sports world at the end of 1987 through misdemeanors—one, almost on the final day of the year. The way these incidents were handled, and the public reaction to them, serves as a reminder of prevailing Japanese societal values.

To a great extent, retribution seemed to be based on the culprits' attitudes subsequent to the event. One, contrite in his confession, was suspended and forced to accept a severe reduction in pay, but he managed to emerge with a degree of public sympathy and his career intact. The other, unrepentant and critical of authority, found himself banished from the sport forever.

The contrasts do not end there: The survivor is a great player, but one in the twilight of his career; the dropout had just risen to the pinnacle of his profession, but with potential unfulfilled. The former is the ace pitcher of the Seibu Lions, Osamu Higashio, who just two months before his temporary fall from grace contributed mightily toward his team's victory in the six-game Japan Series against the Yomiuri giants.

Higashio's sin was to have been caught gambling at mahjongg in a friend's apartment. My first reaction to this piece of news was, "So what?" In Australia, if we arrested those who played poker for money in someone's home, there wouldn't be enough room in the jails. However, it turned out that the friend kept bad company, and one of the players at the mahjongg table happened to be a *yakuza* (an underground personality).

Many years before Seibu took over, Higashio's team had been shaken by a notorious game-throwing scandal involving gangsters. Higashio, who at that time was still young and not involved, was the last active member of the old Lions team, and the stigma remained. Although he was completely exonerated from any *yakuza* connections, and was legally only up for the minor charge of betting in private, the team was left with no choice but to suspend him indefinitely for his indiscretion.

The other malefactor was Futahaguro, only recently elevated to the venerated sumo ranking of *yokozuna* (grand champion). In sumo's closed society, there was such shame at the event that what really transpired remains unclear. But according to press accounts, Futahaguro got into a verbal tiff with Tatsunami, the boss of his stable, and stormed out in a huff, brushing aside the master's diminutive wife. Unfortunately for both parties, what may have been a minor gesture in the ring resulted in injury to the wife of the stable master.

Unlike Higashio, Futahaguro not only remained unrepentant, but actually criticized his boss's attitude toward sumo—behavior unthinkable for a Japanese. And nowhere outside the world of sumo is discipline more strictly maintained. With a swiftness that would have brought envy to the heart of any major league manager who has had to suffer the insubordination of a star player, Futahaguro was expelled forever. His stable master was also held accountable and penalized by the Association. In the long history of sumo, Futahaguro will go down as one of the two grand champions to have brought disgrace to his status; the other, Wajima, had his stock in the Sumo Association hocked to a *yakuza* by his in-laws, and was also expelled.

Actually, Futahaguro's temperament had already been responsible for the creation of an earlier crisis: In another unprecedented happening, six of his retainers, assigned to look after him, bolted from the stable to protest his physical brutality. But on that occasion, Futahaguro managed to emerge with only a reprimand. The difference in this case is that the action was toward his subordinates, and in sumo's feudalistic world, such behavior is normally tolerated.

Regrettably, Futahaguro was a bully and his protestations concerning his boss sound hypocritical. This may explain why he had no defenders. However, the essential difference between Higashio and Futahaguro is that the former readily acknowledged the primacy of the group and confirmed his willingness to abide by its rules; the latter, on the other hand, challenged the group—and found himself on the outside in short order. The Higashio and Futahaguro cases are reminders that fundamental societal values are slow to change despite all the facile discussions on the lifestyles of the *shinjinrui* (new generation).

ALL A MATTER OF STYLE

OF THE MANY THINGS said about Japan and the Japanese, there would be almost unanimous agreement that a premium is placed on manners—exceptions are in public places and when traveling in groups, etc.—and that Japanese is a difficult language. The former compounds the latter, as I found out very quickly in my earlier career here.

After an absence of some twenty years from Japan—during which my use of the language was negligible—I was hired abroad in 1965 to help set up the current shop here. I cannot deny that my competency in Japanese had something to do with my hiring, since its combination with qualifications in market research in the West was non-existent in those days.

Excessive Politeness is Not Good

Any who progress beyond the structural difficulties of the Japanese language know that areas which few foreigners penetrate are the various styles of speaking that are required for individual circumstances. Japanese was not a foreign tongue to me, so back in the mid-1960s, I went about showing off my prowess; while I was certainly impressing my non-Japanese associates, on hindsight perhaps I was alienating some of my Japanese colleagues. This was revealed to me over saké and *yakitori*—one of the Japanese occasions in which we encounter open truths about ourselves—when I was told that the trouble with my Japanese was that it was too polite at times. I must hurriedly point out that this is a problem with native speakers and that it is still better for the average foreigner to err on the side of politeness.

While Americans and Australians lack the art, some older Western cultures can be linguistically polite and rude at the same time. The Japanese actually have a word—*ingin burei*— for "polite-rudeness." But my Japanese colleague was not referring to that, either, since it would have been clear that I had no intention to put down other people. It was a very subtle issue, hard to explain in words.

Recently, the *Asahi Shimbun* headlined; "The abuse of honorifics must stop." Takao Suzuki, a distinguished commentator, berated NHK (Japan Broadcasting Corporation) for its lack of linguistic discipline. Many examples were given, but to quote just one: "To say to the viewers that Sakurai-*san*, a fellow announcer, has returned from China is an abuse of the honorific *san*. The habit of attaching *san* to someone in one's company when talking to outsiders is now routine and normal. Are those responsible at NHK for letting this practice continue allowed to remain unquestioned?" The subject, to an "outsider," would seem not to warrant the extensive space the *Asahi* devoted to it. It was important because the matter went beyond that of correct use of language.

Topsy-Turvy Situation

Quite separately, in a letter to the paper, a housewife complained that she heard a call over a public address system of a preparatory school saying, "So-and-so sensei (teacher), please come immediately as your *seito* (pupil)-*san* has arrived." She commented wryly that perhaps at a prep school, the student was more important than the teacher. The social ranking was confused with the simple use of *san*.

In the West, too, we don't normally introduce our wives with the prefix Mrs., since she is family. This rule extends in Japan to anyone in the company, since they are family too. So don't introduce any Japanese in your company, even if he is your superior, as *san*. Irrespective of his objective status in the community, through you, he is always inferior to anyone outside the company.

There was a time when strong claims in advertising for the product's superiority over others were rare, perhaps because it was like affixing a *san* to something you produced. As a result, the Japanese have developed their own style of presenting product benefits, sometimes too subtle for the obtuse foreigner. Advertisements that bluntly state the product's strengths seem to be on the increase, and this may be consistent with the tendency observed above on the breakdown in linguistic protocol. It seems that some products are even referred to now with the equivalent of *san*!

So I never thought that I would again see the day that the subject of comparative advertising—the kind where your product is compared with a competitor's to demonstrate its superiority—would be seriously debated in Japan. But the Fair Trade Commission's 1987 announcement that this type of advertising may now be allowed, provided that certain guidelines are followed, stirred debate. Yes, again—for the issue was taken up quite seriously in the mid-1960s. I arrived in·Japan in late 1965 to set up a pre-testing system for TV commercials, a field which we pioneered here. Comparative advertising was called the "Brand X" approach then; you didn't actually name your competitor but implied it.

Who's Protecting Whom?

It may surprise Western readers today to learn that the first request to examine the effectiveness of comparative advertising in 1966 came from two Japanese advertisers. The Western advertisers were all assured by their Japanese staff that this approach wouldn't work in Japan, so few were attempting it. The key to this is style; some American-style advertising is unacceptable in the United Kingdom and vice versa. But it is often possible to put over the same concept, while adapting to local tastes. It is theoretically possible to have a Japanese style of comparative advertising. But most in the 1960s seemed to miss this point.

One advertiser having no such hang-up was a major Japanese electric appliance company. The other was a Japanese brewery. The former had a new model vacuum cleaner for which they could confidently display the suction power over existing ones. The advertising department desperately wanted to demonstrate this fact, and the best way to do it was through comparative advertising. In deference to the social code that precluded overtly knocking the competition, they did this by comparing the new model with their own existing model. Coins were lined up on the edge of the tatami floor with a split screen comparison of the suction efficacy.

The consumers viewing the ad did not object to this approach, and, in fact, our research showed that there was a significant shift toward the advertised brand among viewers. Diagnostic data showed that although the advertiser was demonstrating a comparison within his own product range, most viewers thought that it also applied to competitive brands. So here it seemed we had a successful Japanese comparative advertisement. However, the commercial was never aired. The advertisers' association ruled that it represented covert criticism of the competition and, thus, was disharmonious to business. Senior management was anxious not to rock the industrial boat and the advertising department shrugged and went back to the much less direct route favored by the business community.

It struck me then that the code was protecting the manufacturers rather than the consumer; the consumer was denied an essential piece of information for selecting a vacuum cleaner. Obviously, it was more important to protect domestic industrial harmony, and things haven't changed. Recently, we've had a consumer association conducting a blind taste test of Japanese rice versus imported rice, triumphantly stating that the former was much preferred. The self-appointed protectors of the consumer were suggesting that this was another reason that rice should not be imported. Research of this kind, of course, makes no sense as it omits price. Some consumers in the actual marketplace may be prepared to sacrifice quality if the price were substantially less. Anyway, nobody raised objections to this "comparative advertising" that "protected" the domestic industry from imports.

Let the Consumer Decide

Comments on the subject of "comparative advertising" in 1986 are confused and many still show a contempt of the consumer's good sense. One newspaper article carried the subheadline, "Differences in ad appeal make Japanese skeptical of comparing brands." In the very first paragraph, the writer said that a recent comparative ad "could become a standard among advertisers in Japan," — a seeming contradiction. A senior manager for a Western brand was quoted (perhaps out of context) as saying that comparative advertising would be useful "because Japanese hesitate to buy foreign products." (His brand commands a 70% share of the category!) He wanted to compare his product with another product category, so it had nothing to do with Japanese consumer nationalism. And a creative director of a Japanese advertising agency said that "since Japanese don't like to attack rivals so blatantly, these kinds of advertisements will give consumers a bad image of the sponsor." He modified this, however, in reference to style, noting that ads of this type will spread as long as the competitive brand is not identified. As I always say, let the consumer decide. In any society, most advertisers would hesitate to run ads that are considered to be in bad taste. The consumer does not need to be protected in this matter.

Some Commercials Travel Poorly

Back to style. It was virtually an American political commerical for local consumption, showing some U.S. congressmen smashing Toshiba-brand products. However, this being the information age, the images were quickly flashed across Japanese screens. Although I claim to be bi-cultural, I missed the fundamental offense perceived by many of my Japanese colleagues. Frankly, I thought that here were a bunch of adults making idiots of themselves.

When I appeared on a TV talk program soon after, the discussion

centered on the culpability of Toshiba's selling of submarine pro-
peller equipment to the Soviet Union, thus endangering allied security, as had been clearly acknowledged by a noted authority. In fact,
the Prime Minister himself had referred to that act as treachery.
Chatting afterwards, I was startled by the vehemence of the remark
made by a member of the production staff: "Regardless of the
wrong committed, those sledge-hammering scenes just piss me off."

A few days later, there was a letter in a Japanese morning
newspaper from a high-school boy. "They were acting like a bunch
of kids," he wrote—echoing my sentiments. However, he went further: "It is regrettable that representatives of a country which is supposed to be a world leader should behave in this way." I thought to
myself that the Japanese concern for matter of style is what distracts
them from the central issue.

In this respect, things haven't changed despite all the talk about a
changing Japan and the *shinjinrui* (new generation). Countless times I
have had to explain to a Western client that the manner of presentation in his advertisement was getting in the way of properly communicating his concept.

With the perception of "Japan bashing," the committed
"violence" has been viewed as extending to all Japanese products,
not just to those of Toshiba. Once seen in this light, the imagery is
quite savage and lacking in humanity. While the two cannot be compared for the magnitude of the insult, an American seeing the Stars
and Stripes burned in the streets of Teheran would react in the same
way. To one Japanese commentator, the scenes brought back
memories of war years when children were shown sticking bamboo
spears into the national flags of the Allies. Oceans of blood were
spilled at the time and such passions were expected—and much more
understandable.

Intellectually, Japan's large trade surplus and the semiconductor dispute should have been separated from the Toshiba affair. However, emotionally they clearly were not. The Toshiba incident could not have happened at a worse time, as it raised the issue of national security and aided those who promote Japan as the chief villain. To most foreigners who live and work in Japan, this positioning is absurd.

The most disturbing aspect is that some Japanese are now imputing racist attitudes to the U.S. We did not see scenes of Kongsburg's products—the Norwegian company that was also indicted—being smashed alongside Toshiba's. The obscene remark by a U.S. politician that he agreed with the decision of Harry S. Truman to drop the atom bomb on Japan but only regretted that a few more were not dropped, were duly reported by the Japanese press. I wonder what the U.S. reaction would have been if a similar remark had been made about Pearl Harbor?

Many will remember the *New York Times* article by the late Theodore White—the distinguished American journalist—in which he said that Japan was doing to the United States what it failed to accomplish in Pearl Harbor, but that this time Japan was sending over VCRs and cars instead of bombs. The comment insulted the American consumer, since, unlike bombs, Japanese products have crossed the oceans because they were wanted.

The buzzword in my business until fairly recently was "global" marketing. Now we talk about global economy. The smashing scenes of Toshiba products are certainly not appropriate as global advertising and they are certainly not helping the global economy. Japanese commentators suggested that perhaps they should retaliate by showing scenes of herbicide contaminated Winston Light cigarettes—a case reported widely here—being smashed by endangered

Japanese consumers. (The logical Western response would be to point out that one can hardly place a matter of hazards to selected individuals in the same dimension as one that threatens a whole nation).

The commentator then had second thoughts and said that a better commerical would be simply to pause with the hammer in midair and then smile—an approach that would hardly work in the United States. A close Japanese colleague used to caution me when my Australian temper got the better of me: "Fields-san, the one that shows his emotions is the loser." The sledge-hammer approach seldom works in Japanese advertising.

PART THREE

UNIQUENESS, IDIOSYNCRACIES, OR JUST EXCUSES?

That Annoying Claim to Uniqueness

Japan's Self-Analysis Going too Far?

JAPANOLOGISTS SHOULD BE CALLED "Japanapologists." No, this is not the opinion of one frustrated at his lack of success in the Japanese market. It was Ivan Hall writing in the *Asian Wall Street Journal*, himself a Japanologist.

Hall feels that the many treatises on Japan, although serving some purpose in the past as antidotes to "Occupation-bred Yankee arrogance," now merely inhibit Japan's internationalization. The Japanese tendency to narcissistic self-analysis was attacked earlier by Roy Andrew Miller in his 1982 book, *Japan's Modern Myth.*

It reminded me of a delightful evening on the Sumida River, in an old fashioned *yakata-bune* (houseboat), the climax of which was spectacular fireworks; everyone enthusiastically absorbed the "unique" Japanese mood.

Overwhelmed, my young neighbor exclaimed, "I'm really glad I was born a Japanese!" but then glanced at me and said, "I'm sorry, Fields-san!" Absolutely no malice intended, of course, and certainly no offense taken, as I offered my usual foreign smile kept for many such occasions.

It made me wonder, though, why Americans, British, and Australians don't keep congratulating themselves for who they are while having fun. Of course, there are royal occasions for the British, July 4th events for the Americans, and Anzac Day for the Australians, but these are national ceremonies in which the blood is supposed to stir and national awareness is expected.

The Japanese are being trapped in their own "uniqueness" syndrome. Karel van Woferen's *The Japan Problem* and Peter Drucker's *Adversarial Trade* argue essentially that if that is the case, Japan should be excluded from international rules that apply to other advanced countries.

All cultures have some unique aspects and the world is better for that. But the Japanese seem to prefer that their uniqueness is comprehensible only to themselves. So an "industry" has been spawned to expound the significance of Japanese being different from everybody else.

Hall quotes Glen Fukushima of the U.S. Trade Office as saying that "If you're a foreigner who is too critical about Japan, your sources of information, funding, or friends dry up." Thus, old Japan-hands turn into "Japanapologists," arguing that Japan's insistence on being different should be tolerated. There are cases where this applies, but as a general statement it approaches a slur and in itself displays a dangerous tendency.

Mind you, I'm not being defensive. Writing in Japanese, I tend to include the Western viewpoint, and vice versa when in English, so I have few friends left anyway. I will still stick to my often stated contention that ignoring differences in cultural values is courting disaster in the marketplace. In no way is this an apologia.

Japanologist or "Japanapologist," "hired foreign hand" or "Japan basher?" The skies are becoming unfriendly for the students of both cultures. Perhaps a little less self-indulgence on the Japanese side will make the international skies somewhat more friendly.

In Search of an Aidentiti

However, if self-analysis is not merely narcissistic but leads to a clear understanding of Japan's position in the international community, then nothing but good can come from it. A gala symposium was held in July 1987 at the Imperial Hotel to launch a new think tank, an arm of Dentsu, the giant advertising agency.

Called Dentsu Soken, it is headed by Naohiro Amaya, the doyen of Japan's internationalizing efforts, who continues to speak out on Japan's needs in this respect. The theme of the symposium was "In Search of a Japanese Identity" but "identity" was spelled in katakana as aidentiti. So the sponsors had decided that a foreign-derived word would be more appropriate to describe this very significant Japanese quest.

A little later, then prime Minister Yasuhiro Nakasone chose "The Establishment of a Japanese Identity" as the title of his talk for a summer seminar held at Karuizawa by his ruling party.

While Dentsu was still exploring, the prime minister was on more secure grounds, except that he, too, had to use the word aidentiti. It was at such a seminar that Mr. Nakasone made his now notorious remarks about the advantage of a racially pure society. He is obviously unconcerned about language purity.

Both these events highlight a familiar problem in cross-cultural advertising. It starts when the Western head office insists on an international campaign and asks the hapless advertising manager at the branch to make sure that the copy is the same. Insistence on back translations does not necessarily help when there just isn't a Japanese equivalent expression. Half the time, the foreign reader does not know that the translator has cheated by just using *katakana*, creating a word that probably the consumer didn't understand at first.

Never mind; by the time the head office wakes up to the fact, although that's the exception, the word has probably passed into the Japanese language through the advertising, providing quite a panache for the product. The copywriter has walked away with a prize or two for his creativity, which all came about because originally he couldn't find the right Japanese word.

When a well-used word in one culture doesn't exist in the other, it could signify important differences in values. My two favorites are *puraibashii* or "privacy," a concept which did not exist in Japan until recently, and *shakaijin*, which translates as "social being" or "public person," but is what a Japanese boy becomes when he gets a job or a girl when she gets married. So I went to the most authoritative English-Japanese dictionary to see how I could translate "identity" into Japanese.

For the first definition, my back translation will come out as "to be exactly the same, to be under identical conditions, congruences." No, that can't be right for either Dentsu Soken or Mr. Nakasone. So let's try the other definition: "to be the same person, to be genuninely that person." I quickly gave up as a translator and settled for *aidentiti*. So now a new Japanese word is born and proceeds to be defined through the context in which it is used.

As a matter of fact, the word is probably now in use because it became a marketing buzzword fairly recently. Americans thought that they had discovered the concept of "corporate identity" but the

Japanese have been savvy to it for some time. They loved the idea of giving it a label, that is, *kōporēto aidentiti* — which really is closer to the active phrase, "corporate image building" in the Japanese context. Immediately, a CI boom was created.

The absence of the word "identity" in the Japanese culture until now is not really surprising. If you belong to a homogeneous society and to the same village, as Mr. Nakasone said earlier, then you don't have to go around explaining yourself to others. In fact, a distinct identity can be a problem, as attested by the well-worn Japanese saying, "The nail that protrudes gets whacked on its head." Lately, the group non-identity syndrome has produced a new hit saying — "I'm not scared of going against the red light if I'm with everybody." Internationally, Japan has become a protruding nail and is now being criticized for ignoring the red light. So there is a need for Japan itself to search for an international identity.

Does the Japanese "Mind-Set" Reject Foreign Products?

In early 1986, the Danforth whirlwind passed through the island nation of Japan. The Republican senator had been pressing retaliatory measures against Japan on the charge of unfair trade practices. Interestingly, the event was not called *shokku* (shock) as was the case with Nixon's soybean embargo or the OPEC price rise. A whirlwind passes but a shokku remains.

The Japanese rolled out the red carpet for this vociferous critic of Japanese ways, with everybody from the prime minister down listening to the senator's words and nodding. Several Japanese dignitaries were quoted as saying that Sen. Danforth made some important points that should be noted carefully. The papers ran a profile of the

Senator as a lay preacher with very sincere beliefs. The Japanese penchant for avoiding confrontational situations was on full display.

This was before the word "Japan-bashing," emanating from the U.S., became a common Japanese phrase. Everybody here feels put-upon now. It was also before the Gephardt trade bill amendment, so the Danforth name has receded into the background in 1988. However, the view Sen. Danforth represents seems still to be in vogue. I am sure that through formal Japanese meals in a *ryōtei* (a traditional Japanese restaurant, the expenses of which would allow the average New Yorker to go to London and back for dinner) and visits to the culturally rich area of Kamakura, there was a concerted effort to convince him that Japan was very different from the United States and that this applied to ways of doing business. A loud sigh accompanies the plea that it was not any conspiracy on the part of Japanese business that made some U.S. firms' paths rocky and oh, if only the Americans could understand that it was due to the difference in cultures. The trouble with this line of thought is that the senator agrees with this proposition.

What the Japanese people so often imply, with a certain smugness, is that the Japanese culture is so unique that it is unfathomable to the Westerner. In which case, why should Americans make the effort, and Sen. Danforth would be quite right in saying that "The ball is in your court. Do something about it or else."

On these tacks, it is pretty certain that neither side is going to get very far. On the other hand, if Sen. Danforth is totally right, as his fundamentalist bent takes him, it is bad news for those of us who are non-Japanese and who are working in Japan. How do you go about changing a culture overnight?

Sen. Danforth is often quoted as saying that the Japanese have a mind-set that rejects foreign products. Since I often have problems with those who insist that the Japanese consumers are becoming Americanized, the statement at least has a ring of novelty. My Japanese friend serves me Nescafé; in his bathroom are a Schick razor, Lux toilet soap, and Timotei shampoo. He lit up a Lark after his coffee, with a Dunhill lighter. His wife had Del Monte ketchup and Rama margarine on the table and she had just changed the baby's Pampers. The eldest boy came home from school, changed into his Levi's and said he was going out with his friends to have a Big Mac. He needed money for a Coke, too. Giving him extra money she asked him to bring back some Kentucky Fried Chicken. None of that for Sen. Danforth, to whom the Japanese consumers are just a bunch of nationalistic bigots who reject anything that is foreign. She, by the way, is an Avon Lady.

Unlike the assertion that the Japanese consumers are becoming Westernized, Sen. Danforth's proposition is easier to disprove than prove on simply observed evidence. Of course, if you asked a Japanese consumer whether Japanese products were superior, he or she would answer in all probability, "It all depends," which may not suit the senator's absolutist principles, but it would be the correct answer. My ex-boss in Australia headed the "Buy Australia" campaign. When he invited executives to his room after 5:00, he offered them British Scotch. His overcoat came from Saville Row and he was driven to work in an American Pontiac. He believed sincerely in promoting Australian products but knew, as a consumer, that this did not apply to all products. The average consumer buys something that he perceives to have an appropriate cost-benefit relationship, be it intangible. In this sense, the Japanese consumers are no different from their American or Australian counterparts.

In the course of our business, we interview thousands of Japanese consumers each month, but the source of the product is often unknown. Reputations and reliability are, of course, highly relevant, and it is true that some countries, sometimes unfairly, have image problems in this respect. In the case of a certain top American food brand, we found that the buyers were spit fairly equally between those who either: (a) thought that the product was made in the U.S. and marketed by a well-known Japanese company, or (b) thought that it was a U.S. brand made under license to the same company, or (c) were unsure whether to think (a) or (b). We found no evidence that this difference in perception had a significant influence on the purchasing decision, although the association with a reputable Japanese company did help. However, it was not the fact that the company was Japanese that helped *per se*, but because it was well-known and provided a sense of reliability which is consistent with Japanese cultural attitudes toward authority. It has nothing to do with xenophobia. Importantly, the research showed that the brand under the Japanese company's label would have been a no-no. The key product attributes were more consistent with qualities associated with the West.

The perception that the Japanese consumer has a peculiar anti-foreign mind-set dampens the efforts of foreign marketers—the "why bother" syndrome—and doesn't serve Sen. Danforth's ultimate objective one iota. Anyway, it is just not true.

Playing by Some Japanese Rules

The climate has changed since Sen. Danforth's visit in 1986, indicated by two speeches given December 1988, in Tokyo, to quite different audiences and on quite different subjects. The one I attended was addressed by none other than Akio Morita, the chairman of

Sony, to a packed house at an American Chamber of Commerce luncheon, ostensibly on Japanese investments in the United States. The other was by James Fallows, the eminent journalist of the *Atlantic* magazine who was in town lecturing on effective writing to the business community. If it wasn't for the fact that I was too old to do anything about it, I would have canceled my appointment to hear him.

While an unlikely event, it would be interesting to have Fallows on the same platform as Morita. Morita lamented that some of the rules governing American business behavior created self-inflicted wounds that worsened trade tensions between Japan, while Fallows has despaired that Japan, would ever accept rules based on American beliefs. But Morita bluntly posed the question: Should all the rules come from the Unitrd States?''

Fallows is a staunch believer in free trade, which he equates with American values; his hard hitting article in the September 1987 issue of the *Atlantic* was titled ''Japan - Playing by Different Rules.'' It is a classic of its kind, together with Peter Drucker's well-known piece in the *Wall Street Journal* that charged Japan with ''adversarial trade'' and Karen van Wolferen's ''Japan Problem'' in *Foreign Affairs.* Drucker saw Japan as mercantilist and thus differentiated it from West Germany, which had an even greater export volume. Wolferen saw the rules of Japanese political decision-making to be so different from the West's that diplomatic discourse was impossible. Fallows stated: ''In the U.S. economy the consumer is sovereign: in the Japanese the producer is.'' From their respective perspectives, all three implied that the twain shall never meet, since differences were rooted in culture. Japan will have to be left out of the Western game because she played by different rules.

I once quoted them to a study group of younger Japanese

parliamentarians, saying that while this scenario was unlikely because of businesses' global interdependence, Japanese rules will have to be modified to narrow the differences, if Japan was to continue trading as freely as now. The chairman, Kotaro Tawara, well-known as a maverick, asked sharply, "But who makes the rules?" Caught off guard, I answered lamely, "Historically, the stronger side, I suppose." It was a poor answer to a good question, but fortunately he let it rest. One of the points made by Morita was that rules were made to be compatible with societal values and too radical a departure spelled trouble and therefore Americans should be patient. I can hear the chorus of "but we have waited long enough!" to this standard Japanese response.

However, there has been a subtle shift in emphasis in the on-going debate. Clyde Prestowitz argues in a 1988 book *Trading Places* that Americans cannot expect Japan to change its rules. Taking a different tack to Messrs. Drucker, Wolferen and Fallows, he proposes that, to meet the Japanese challenge, America has to adopt some of the Japanese rules. Is this the beginning of the end to the strong belief that only American rules should ultimately prevail?

Morita said as much although he is hardly in the same camp as Mr. Prestowitz. He felt that unless the United States brought some of its current rules more in line with those of Japan, friction would continue because Japan holds the stronger cards. For example, Mr. Morita observed that some of the anti-trust regulations in the United States are counter productive. Of course, it was wrong for competitors to get together and fix prices but other types of competitive alliances should be feasible. Only the large could afford to invest in some kinds of developments. He felt that Americans were handicapping themselves with too stringent an application of anti-trust rules.

In 1987, Fallows concluded his article thus: "The Japanese have made a choice for their society, and we should make one for ours. That's better than thinking that we can talk the Japanese into behaving more like us, or relying on 'free trade' to reach equilibrium.'' Morita said, toward the end of his speech, that as practical businessmen, "we have no time to bash each other" and that there was something in the air for greater cooperation.

In both Japan and Europe, businessmen are modifying their rules to accommodate the so-called globalization. "Globalization," like Fallows' "free trade," will never come into perfect being. But businesses cannot afford to ignore even a modified contingency and their combined actions of greater accommodation with the other's rules are creating a trend. While some Americans may despair that Japan will never adopt all their rules, the fact of the matter is that changing the rules is not a one-sided affair.

ARE EATING HABITS NO LONGER JAPANESE?

From East/West to West/East—A Shift in Balance

THE FOOD INDUSTRY CENTER has conducted a survey on primary and junior high-school children's eating habits. What emerges is a rather sad picture in which the children are hounded from one activity to another with little time for personal fun. They are indeed busy with "extracurricula school activities" (85.7%), "going to culture-related lessons, for example, piano, calligraphy, etc." (43.3%), "going to tutorial schools" (39.6%), and "going to sports classes" (25.1%). Slightly over half (53.9%) feel they "don't get enough sleep," with a significant minority (39.2%) "sometimes burning the midnight candle."

While the above data suggests that school children may be somewhat skimped for time, the survey does not provide any evidence that their nutritional needs are being neglected. Preference is solidly for meat over fish at a ratio of 2 to 1. Lest we jump to the usual pat rationalization that the new generation is becoming

Americanized in their food habits, an overwhelming 72.8% preferred rice over bread. Still, their favorite dishes were "things like hamburgers and fried chicken that you can eat with your fingers." The converse was true for fish, leading to the unpopularity of "fish with small bones, because they were bothersome to eat." Westernization is certainly in progress.

As for the adults, a good look was taken by the Ministry of Agriculture in its *Food Monitor* in September 1986. On the positioning of the daily meal, respondents voted mostly for "an opportunity for a balanced nutritional intake" (61.7%), with practically all the rest seeing it as "an opportunity to enrich family life through the sharing of the meal occasion" (37.2%). Understandably, there was a tendency for the older respondents to go even more for the former and the younger and the working housewife to go for the latter.

When given a choice of various attitudes toward Japanese versus Western dishes, despite the highly loaded expression "suitable for a Japanese" (*Nihonjin rashii*), the great majority indicated a total lack of concern for such a distinction.

Since we suspect a bias toward the expected answer—respondents could hardly express a lack of concern for "nutritional balance"—let us just say that from the consumer's perception, the Japanese/Western distinction as applied to food is becoming increasingly irrelevant. Conclusive proof of this was supplied when respondents were asked to define "Japanese-style food life": an overwhelming 77.8% picked "a balanced combination of traditional meals of rice, miso soup, pickles, and fish, with other foods such as meats and dairy products." Only 14.3% selected "traditional meals of rice, etc."

From Store-Bought to Home-Baked Bread

The *Nikkei Keizai Shimbun* (The Japan Economic Journal) nominated the "Automatic Bread Maker" as the hit product of 1987. The flour millers, languishing in what seemed a mature market, had been revitalized. On the other hand, bakeries were unhappy. Nothing illustrates more dramatically that, in Japan, consumer demand can be pulled by a newfangled appliance. Few Japanese commentators seem to realize that the popularity of this device is due to its being an extension of the Japanese food culture. After all, hot rice has always been served for breakfast. So why not hot bread? (Like their penchant for white rice, the Japanese also overwhelmingly prefer white bread for breakfast).

Most appliance stores are in the vertical network of a major manufacturer. This means that if one manufacturer comes out with a new hit product, the stores in another chain fear that sales will be lost to competing neighboring ones and thus they must be placated as quickly as possible by each manufactuter who rushes out with a similar product. Thus, a boom in new appliances is created even more quickly than in most other countries, filling the shelves of approxmiately 70,000 appliance stores.

I cannot help remembering a similar boom that occurred several years ago with the *mochi* (rice cake) making device. More than 1 million units of this appliance were sold in two years but the boom soon passed and the current sales level is about half of the peak. However, it is dangerous to push this analogy too far. *Mochi* is not an item that is made daily—its consumption peaks solidly around the new year—and equipment that is not used regularly tends to finish up a forgotten item in the cupboard. In contrast, since rice is cooked almost everyday, the automatic rice maker still commands an enormous market of about 6.5 million unit sales a year.

Although volume sales of store bread have flattened, bread is still served regularly for breakfast in many homes. So rice is a better reference point than *mochi* for the automatic bread maker. Just like the rice cooker, the bread maker is set before going to bed, readying the item for hot consumption on arising.

It was felt that the home baking of bread may even stimulate the market for bread as a whole; bakeries have traditionally provided fresh, daily baked breads to the home, and some consumers will be reminded of the fact. The chief sufferers could be the branded breads in supermarkets. But expectations for the long-term prospects of the automatic bread maker were not all rosy. The working housewife—a new force in the market—is increasingly voting for convenience. Will she get tired of taking the flour mix out of the package, measuring the water, setting the time, and pushing the button? Convenience versus home-baked goodness. A whole industry awaited the ultimate outcome, with baited breath and crossed fingers. Well, the direction reversed much sooner than expected and this could be the shortest boom and bust on record. The industry that bullishly predicted that 40 percent of homes would own the Bread Maker found that sales had peaked very rapidly. In fact, at the end of 1988, against sales of approximately one million units in 1987, the industry was estimating its sales for the year at a measly 300,000. For once, Japanese industry's penchant for rushing out with the earliest indication of success to create a genre seems to have backfired.

In the first place, the sheer novelty of having freshly baked bread in one's own kitchen generated enormous initial word-of-mouth, which led to curiosity buying. However, the fun soon wore off and boredom set-in. After all, it was only unique just after it was baked, first thing in the morning, and after that the bread was not as good as the professionally produced ones from the local bakery. Anyway, it was going against the current trend among housewives for convenience; the automatic rice cooker does provide that attribute. On hindsight, it seems hardly worth the bother of preparation on the previous night. It takes up space in the small Japanese kitchen and worse still, when it switches itself on during the early hours of the morning, makes a racket that can be heard in the not so far away bedroom. While some manufacturers are putting on a stiff upper lip, saying that the bugs are being ironed out and that the true potential is yet to be tested, hindsight research suggests that there will be fewer brands on the market in the near future.

Beef in the Japanese Food Culture

A letter in the *Wall Street Journal* states: "[various commentators] must stop assuming there are traditional or culturally unique reasons, as the Japanese ceaselessly aver - or any justification at all — for Japan's markets to remain as closed as they are." The writer was referring to the construction industry. Beef and oranges are the most immediate pressure points for the liberalizing of the Japanese market and one is reminded of the famous remark by a senior Japanese government official that, since the Japanese have longer intestines than Westerners, beef is not a suitable food for them! As there is some legitimate ground for saying that the Japanese lead the world in average life expectancy because of their diet, it is a wonder somebody hasn't come up with the argument that foreign food imports will threaten Japanese longevity, joining those who warn of the health hazards resulting from the use of herbicides and additives in imported foods.

For beef, though, the main concern is that the livelihood of some fellow Japanese are threatened through imports but, unlike rice, the industry cannot claim special cultural privileges. Although legend has it that in ancient days beef was served to the Emperor, there is no evidence in historical documents that beef was popularly consumed in pre-modern Japan. With the advent of Buddhism, the consumption of meat was officially banned in 676. Wild boar, venison and bear were sometimes consumed under the guise of therapy, but the general population developed an abhorrence of four-legged beasts as unclean creatures. This attitude spilled over to unfortunates who dealt with them such as in tanning, which created an under class who were discriminated against.

The first exposure to beef as a food concept was with the arrival of the trading and evangelizing Spanish and Portuguese in the 16th century. It is on record that Lord Takayama, who was converted to Christianity, entertained the Lords Gamou and Hosokawa in 1590, at a feast in which beef was served. The fact that the dish — probably Spanish — deliberately challenged prevailing social norms is interesting; the serving of beef was almost a proof of conversion to the West.

However, this flirtation with the West was very short-lived, since Japan subsequently entered a long period of isolation. It was not that beef totally disappeared as a food — the exceptional Hikone clan annually presented it pickled in miso to the shogunate, and Dutch meat recipes were served in the controlled port of Nagasaki. But for all intents and purposes, the populace remained ignorant of beef eating until the arrival of Commodore Perry's black ships in 1854 heralded an influx from the West.

In this period, Yukichi Fukuzawa, the founder of Keio University and one of the intellectuals who encouraged the modernizing of Japan, had already recommended beef as a food. As with the early Lord Takayama, beef seems almost to be a symbol of Westernizing influences. The few foreigners who had arrived toward the end of the rule of the Shogun had to import their meat from afar, but to save costs, the Tajima breed of cows was transported to Yokohama from the Kobe area — the origin of the popular Kobe beef. The first slaughteryard was established in Shirogane in Tokyo's Minato Ward in 1866 to supply the expatriate community. So it was the foreign consumer who created the first market for Kobe Beef; so much for the argument that it came into being to accommodate the uniquely discriminating Japanese palate!

A strong case could no doubt have been made that there was no potential for beef in Japan because of Buddhist values. Had market research been available, I am certain that product testing would have shown the average Japanese recoiling from the unaccustomed odor; the simplistic conclusion would have been that there was no market potential for it. However, beef became popular via a dish called *gyunabe* — the precursor of *sukiyaki* — another demonstration of the Japanese genius for adopting a Western concept while insisting on a local execution. The Japanese consumer proved that restrictions imposed from above had little to do with personal inclination and took to beef dishes with a vengeance. What limited its consumption, then as now, was the high cost. This reminds me that twenty years ago, some argued seriously that because of language and other cultural inhibitions, the "average" Japanese was not interested in going overseas! Rather, the lack of allowable dollars kept the market down.

Perhaps historically there was some symbolic importance of beef in

Japanese culture. But modern Japan is no longer concerned with such symbols. The 1988 White Paper on Agriculture analyzes consumer food trends — a contradiction in terms since the analysts themselves control the market through price manipulation. How do we really know what the trend will be under "natural" circumstances? Even then, the Ministry of Agriculture, Forestry and Fisheries is prone to acknowledge a trend toward beef and away from rice — both price controlled. Free of controls and official posturing, a movement toward or away from any product category could produce an unrestrained exponential rate of growth or decline.

IDIOSYNCRACIES IN THE MARKET

The Distribution Bugbear

MUCH OF THE DISCUSSION on Japanese management by outside observers is inevitably superficial in that it is based on the Japanese business elites—the Sonys, the Hondas, the Mitsubishis, etc. It is like talking about American management as though all firms were composed of the IBMs and the Procter & Gambles. Inside observers such as James Abbeglen, the noted scholar and author of *Kaisha* have tried to correct this fallacy. However, the fact remains that representatives of large corporations are the only ones foreign businessmen generally meet. Few Japanese, but many foreigners, would be surprised to know that 96% of manufactuers in Japan employ fewer than 300, and have a registered capital of no more than ¥100 million (about $800,000 in 1988), and that these small firms produce almost half of total manufactured value. But, of course, it is the giants that ultimately assemble, label, and market the final product, so the medium-to-small companies are truly behind the scenes in the manufacturing industry.

A case was given to me by NHK (Japan Broadcasting Corporation) to present in a TV series in late 1987 and early 1988 called "The Anatomy of Japan: Wellsprings of an Economic Power." It concerned a well-known auto manufacturer who had 300 suppliers from whom raw materials were procured, and this relationship was horizontal, just like in the West. But after that, a remarkable vertical relationship unfolded. The raw materials were first passed down to 156 primary subcontractors, who were ultimately responsible for the delivery of parts to the giant. However, these primary subcontractors in turn handed their orders down to the next level of 3,500 secondary subcontractors, who proceeded to turn over minute part manufacturing to an astonishing 10,000 or so backyard operators. The relationship was entirely vertical in that the responsibility of quality control rested at each level and the giant manufacturer controlled only the primary subcontractors. Thus, the more than 10,000 medium-to-small firms never got to meet the big boss. This vertical link forms the basis of the renowned Japanese "just-in-time-delivery" system.

So there is a pyramid beginning with one guy at the top and spreading down to a large base. This is said to be the strength of Japanese manufacturing, which carries a minimum of inventories and controls quality at each stage, and, while I gazed at the pyramid, it seemed strangely familiar. Yes, it was the Japanese distribution relationship turned upside down. In other words, in distribution, if we start from the final point to the customer, the retail outlet, its supply line consists of numerous layers of wholesalers, shrinking in numbers at each level, finishing with the manufacturer or the importer. The trouble with this pyramid is that while it works for the manufacturing sector, in its international competitive advantage, it does not work for the consumer in distribution. In the manufacturing sector, cost is incurred at each process, but there is commensurate value added in turn. In distribution, too, cost is incurred at each process but no value is added to the product. Both manufacturing and distribution share the benefits of inventory control. After that there is a wide divergence—manufacturing obtains the additional benefit of down-the-line quality control, but in distribution that is a non-issue.

The two pyramids do reflect cultural values as they are based on permanent and closed relationships. Most of the subcontractors in manufacturing serve only one customer, and while this is not the case in distribution, nevertheless, the closed-circle principle still applies. This principle in both manufacturing and distribution is a serious inhibitor of the internationalization of Japan and will continue to be a cause of friction. At least in the case of manufacturing, it has created a dynamo for Japan's economic growth. But the benefit of this manufacturing efficiency is not passed on to the Japanese consumers who continued to say well into 1987 that that's OK, since it is for the good of the Japanese community.

Now that the yen is so strong, the Japanese consumers are supposed to be among the richest in the world. But they all know in 1988 that even if the yen is worth ¥125 to the U.S. dollar outside Japan, it is only worth about ¥230 inside. The Japanese consumer is less likely to continue to be so self-sacrificing.

The Japanese Approach to Market Research

I didn't think cultural values would reach into the fundamentals of market research design, but there it is. I owe this insight to a respected bicultural researcher, Kazuko Pfeiffer, with whom I have worked in the past.

A casual remark by Dr. Pfeiffer gave me quite a jolt. She was given the task of reconciling two sets of data produced by different research firms for a European company; we were one and the other, a noted Japanese firm. Our research had been conducted six years earlier and, putting aside the fact that we would have designed it differently now—six years is a long time in market research technology—and that the Japanese firm's was more recent, the data should have been comparable. Dealing with the same subject, ours should have formed the basis of a trend analysis but in substance it didn't; there was great difficulty in reconciling the two sets of data.

At first Dr. Pfeiffer felt that the Japanese data was less organized than ours. The structure and the vertical flow of our design was closer with which she was accustomed in her association with European firms. On the other hand, as she delved into the data produced by the Japanese firm, she realized that there was an awful lot there. "Was there not a way to create a fusion of both approaches?" she mused.

As we discussed the issue, I struck on an analogy: "The differences between the two are like those between a Western meal and a Japanese meal." The Western meal is a course and proceeds very systematically from soup to dessert. Even the drinks are offered in progression from aperitif to wine to liqueur. Western management wants—naturally enough—action-oriented research, and the findings should move systematically toward some sort of bottom line.

In a Japanese home meal setting, many dishes can be put on the table simultaneously and the eater is free to skip from one to another, picking and choosing. Japanese managers may be pattern perceptive, skimming and scanning, and they like lots of data, sometimes seemingly irrelevant to the Western manager. This does not worry them because they don't expect research to provide all the answers. Quite reasonable, although if you pay good money for research, you may question this attitude. Incidentally, compared to Western companies, in general, the Japanese are very stingy on what they pay for research—this may be related to their lower expectations.

Japanese television is marvelous in reporting on seeming daily trivialities that in fact are revealing of the culture. One of these reports concerned the changing table manners of the very young. The camera observed that the kids were no longer eating traditional Japanese meals the way their elders did. No, it wasn't that they ate with knives and forks. The way food was tackled was segmented into two attitude types—there it is, my market rescarcher's bias. One was called *nagara zoku* and the other was *bakkari zoku*. The word *zoku* means "tribe," and the former "tribe" goes with the flow, while the latter concentrates on one thing.

The camera observed how a Japanese breakfast was tackled. All the elders were *nagara* and skipped from one food item to another, but to the amazement of the reporter, some of the Japanese kids polished one item off before moving on! The camera also observed some foreigners struggling with a Japanese breakfast. They were all *bakkari zoku* and tackled one dish at a time—for example, first the miso soup, then moving to the dried fish, etc. One couple, confronted with the remaining bowl of rice, poured soy sauce over it to flavor it. I must admit, with the exception of the bowl of rice, that I consume one dish at a time. Thus, I also belong to the *bakkari zoku*, with Western tendencies. Perhaps it will be pushing the analogy too far if I say that when these *bakkari zoku* kids grow up, they will start demanding Western-style market research.

This subject deserves further attention and the analogy could be extended to speech-making. Cultural nuances—we could go on forever.

Crazy About Gift Giving

The year-end *o-seibo* gift-giving spree produces a frenzied rush of shoppers every year. Whether people will continue to give is not really the question—what should be asked is what they'll give. Nevertheless, I remember that sometime back in the 1960s, the *Asahi Shimbun* rather ponderously editorialized on this "wasteful" custom and wondered whether it was at all necessary: The writer ruminated on some future time when the Japanese people would become more rational and devote their energies to something more constructive than on what to give to whom. Together with other prognostications at the time—such as the *inevitable* reduction in the number of wholesalers or the collapse of the lifetime employment system, neither of which had come about 20 years later—this viewpoint belonged to the realm of wishful thinking. That the Japanese should become more rational, like Westerners, was a refrain from both foreigners and Japanese alike.

Anyway, if there is a trend away from *o-seibo*, the department stores will be in disastrous straits. Gift giving is very much a barometer on how well department stores will fare financially for the year. According to a survey by the Sumitomo Bank, for the year-end gift-giving season in 1985—and while the features changed, the tendency had not for 1987—the average, married salaried worker is committed to non-routine expenses amounting to 2% or so of his income, over the New Year period. In turn, about 22% of this expenditure is used on *o-seibo* gift giving, excluding gifts given to family members. While such devotion to *o-seibo* giving by the humble individual is in itself quite impressive, institutional gift giving is where the real action belongs.

So, enormous effort is expended over just a few months of the year by department stores. There is no major market in the world in which gift giving has such an impact—both on the distribution system and on the consumer. While the "Japanese are unique" claim is tiresome and certainly overdone, this is one aspect in which Japan presents a distinct characteristic to global marketers. But the efforts made by the retailers are not the reason why the custom persists—although it may seem so.

Although Westerners tend to believe in the pleasure of giving, the Japanese are not great givers because they enjoy the act. To believe this is like believing that the Japanese like to work hard; personal enjoyment has very little to do with it. Westerners tend to believe in the pleasure of giving. Anthropological works show that the *exchange* of gifts is a custom not unique to Japan but exists in many primitive societies—and, of course, the West has its Christmas gifts, too. Apparently, it is a gesture meant to indicate that both the giver and the receiver are a part of a tight circle. Receiving and giving involve complicated social rules and moral obligations which bind the participating parties. Since becoming an accepted member of the relevant circle is of major importance for a foreign corporation in Japan, this ritual cannot be dismissed as being anachronistic or primitive. As my philosophy professor used to say, "In the matter of value judgments, one has to agree to disagree."

The types of products given as *o-seibo* have changed over time. However, the essentially utilitarian base remains unchanged. While perfumes, handbags, etc., are major gift items in the West, they are not so for *o-seibo*, since they are too personal to serve as ritualistic gifts. Thus, soap, which is a daily-use item, has been popular—although it seems to be slipping from pre-eminence of late. This slip has not been caused by its being considered less suitable, but partly because most homes are so overstocked with gifted soap that they never have to buy any. The more important reason is that even in gifts, a more individualistic touch is being welcomed.

As a result, food has gained as a category because of the enormous expansion in the varieties available. This is a reflection of changes in the Japanese cuisine, which has been enriched by reducing carbohydrates, namely rice, and enhanced by adding calories in other forms.

Still, there are also elements shared with the West. The *o-seibo* and Chrismas seasons were both originally tied to a religious occasion. It seems a typical case of starting from the same concept but finishing up with a different positioning. For one, there is a group versus individual orientation. And then, the emphasis on execution, which shows in the enormous emphasis placed on the packaging of the gifts in Japan. This is why department stores dominated all categories, with their prestige imparted via their wrapping papers.

Service: The Invisible Element in Marketing

My phone rang very late at night in my hotel room in St. Louis. "Fields-san, we have a problem here." This is the sort of opening gambit that traveling executives dread. "There were cases of food poisoning at last night's focus group discussions." "My God!", I groaned. "Is it serious?" "Fortunately not, but many of our executives will be tied up for the next few days." My Western side immediately came to the fore and I wanted to know what food was the cause in order to establish the area of legal responsibility. It was the *obento*—the boxed food—brought in from a caterer. "Well, it's their responsibility," I cried. Fields-san should know better than that was the tone at the other end. We had clear social obligations and I was suitably contrite at succumbing to the instinct of protecting my position rather than begging for the forgiveness of the unfortunate people, whose only fault had been to accept our invitation.

For the next few days, the temporarily stricken were visited with gifts, and more importantly, with profuse apologies. It was to be expected that our caterer would also act promptly and in fact the president and a senior director of a major corporation visited the respondents and eventually took charge until everybody was well and back at work, in a few days. At no time was there talk between our company or the caterer on possible litigations. Of course, we were legally clean, but that's like travel agents saying to the bereaved families of a crash that it is the airline's responsibility. We know that it doesn't work that way in Japan. Anyway, it seemed that our reputation was enhanced in unexpected quarters. Our interviewers were very pleased at the way our executives behaved and the word among them was that we were a good company to work for. You see, they were the ones that invited the respondents to come to the sessions and their positions would have been untenable if the company on whose behalf they issued the invitation had acted improperly. Everybody was responsible for everybody else.

This experience was in startling contrast to another, which involved a Western airline. (I know, we all have those airline stories.) I was on a trip to the U.S. on an official invitation from one of the U.S. government departments. I understood that I would be upgraded to first-class, on a space available basis, and this indeed was the case until I diverted to Canada and rejoined the airline at one of the U.S. ports. I was issued a first-class boarding pass and duly took my seat. To the surprise of everyone concerned, another passenger turned up with the same seat assignment. There were smiles at this stage, as I transferred to another seat, but lo! and behold, another passenger turned up to claim that seat, too.

There was great consternation while my ticket was examined and I was unceremoniously informed that I would have to transfer to business class as there was no space available. With all the other first-class passengers watching, it was embarrassing, to say the least. I had this boarding pass and I suppose I could have insisted on my rights, although the one weakness was that I had not paid for the ticket myself. My Japanese side prevailed and I shifted to the back without protest. There is really nothing wrong with that, except that I simmered for all the rest of the trip on the manner in which the matter was handled: the airline staff did not seem to care that somebody on the ground had made a mistake or that there was a computer foul-up that caused embarrassment to one of their customers. Contrast this with the previous Japanese experience. The difference was that in the airline's case, the stewardess felt no responsibility for the wrongly issued pass, since the mistake was not hers. I hazard a guess that there would have been profuse apologies from a Japanese stewardess, as she—and others—would have been involved collectively as employees of the airline, and would have assumed responsibility for the error.

When the "Marketing Mix" was propounded back in the 1950s, we learned to consider the interactions of many elements—"product," "price," "sales," "distribution," "packaging," "advertising," etc. But somehow in the original mix, "service" was left out. The idea that even manufacturers are selling a service and not just a product is now well understood, or is it really? Service is not just the specific action of a stewardess in an aircraft or the shop clerk smiling pleasantly at you. It should extend to taking collective responsibility. How this can be effected is a major management problem, and the Japanese and perhaps some other Asian cultures have the edge here.

In the summer of 1986, a distinguished Japanese sat next to me in an aircraft. He said to me quietly; "I have been a charter subscriber to the Japanese edition of *Readers' Digest* since the days of the MacArthur occupation. But the first time I found out that I was not going to receive my March issue was through the Japanese newspapers!" He was clearly hurt that a loyal customer could be treated in such a cavalier manner. I rather suspect that the matter of notifying subscribers was outside the defined jurisdiction for the "specialists" sent in by the *Digest* to close the Japanese operation. Still, the withdrawl was not precipitated overnight.

Then on June 16, 1986, the *Asahi Shimbun* ran a paragraph headed, "Out of print. . . . and leaving behind a dirty patch?" The *Digest* that started its Japanese edition just after World War II boasted a peak circulation of 1.4 million. Unlike other Japanese periodicals, it was unique in being sold by subscription. According to the *Asahi*, many irate subscribers tried to get their money back when the *Digest* withdrew from the market. The *Digest* did run, in its last issue, a private box and telephone number for refunds, but many subscribers were complaining of nonresponse. In fairness to the *Digest*, the union had seized the subscriber list, making it impossible for the company to effect some of the refunds. There are always two sides to a dispute and it is not my intention to berate the *Digest*. Still, a simple postcard, well ahead of the eruption, would have helped. The task of squaring it with the customers could only be performed by the Western management, since the Japanese staff was on notice and was demoralized. I put it down to the "specialization"-prone West for failing to properly provide for a "general" social obligation—since nobody was assigned to that specific task, nobody could be held responsible. It is a catch-22 that hurts innocent non-Japanese companies that are staying on.

ADVERTISING IN JAPAN

(Most of the following was published in 1980 as "Advertising Strategy in Japan" in Dentsu's Japan Marketing/Advertising. For me, it was an important position paper. On re-reading it in January 1988, I found that I had not changed my basic views on this matter. So here it is again, with only one portion changed, a more recent case study being substituted for the original one on the cake mix that could not be made in an automatic rice cooker. The cake-mix story took up a whole chapter in my From Bonsai to Levi's (1983) and does not warrant a repeat. Fortunately, a case emerged in 1987 that fills the bill quite nicely. This chapter is perhaps more for the marketing professional than the others and could therefore be skipped by the non-specialist.)

Let the Seller Beware?

IN DEVELOPING an advertising strategy in Japan, the Western advertiser *seems* to be faced with four basic options. The two polar extremes are: (1) transferring a strategy, successfully executed elsewhere, *in toto,* and (2) leaving it to the local experts, as no foreigner can hope to fathom the intricacies of communicating in another culture. While they are seemingly antipodal, for all intents and purposes they are identical as they both rely on faith — and adherents of either are unlikely to be interested in this article. However, two other options fall in-between, namely: (3) importing an exogenous strategy but executing it with deference to local taste and possible modifications, and (4) developing an endogenous strategy, ground-up, in a way the original strategy was developed.

If indeed "transferrence" versus "local development" were options, then the selection would still seem a matter of faith. Superficial observations over the years suggest that both have been attempted. Unfortunately, there are no statistics on their respective success (or failure) rates and any available data are suitably ambiguous. But it is too much to expect advertising research, generally conducted ad-hoc, to come up with a synthesized theory on advertising strategy. It has not been done elsewhere and it is unlikely to be done validly in Japan.

No such attempt to arbitrate between the options should be made, since my first contention is that the options, too simply posed, raise false issues and distract from the fundamental one. The real issue is not which option to choose but where to start. Having already stated that advertising research is ad hoc and not capable of generalizations, the best I can do now is to proceed on the empirical base of cases observed over the past 20 years or so. The inferences drawn then are only as good as the cases I have encountered, but, with this proviso, let us start with a product that has been successfully marketed in another country and that you want to introduce to Japan.

The "Japan is Different" Syndrome

Of course, Japan is different from any other country and this is a truism to end all truisms. It is a question of time before you will come across it, from resident foreigners and especially from your Japanese colleagues. Then you may fall for options (1) or (2), that is, "Don't give me that nonsense, it's worked in seven other countries and I've heard that argument in all seven" or "Let's select a Japanese partner that has been successful in his own ways and leave everything to him." Unfortunately, to accept either of these propositions is not to start at all, especially if it leads to emotional rejection of the local culture or blind delegation of responsibility to your local partners.

Before you let the "Japan is different" camp run amok—which includes old Japan hands, as much as your Japanese colleagues—consider whether there is a "need" for your product in Japan, either overt or latent. If there is, then the basis of the need, even if latent, should be your starting point. Now, you may well find that the rationale for your product is indeed different, requiring a fundamental revision of your previous strategy, and I know of many cases that fit this situation. I know many more, however, where the differences were in detail—not in concept but more in execution.

I heard a rueful remark recently from an American client that his particular campaign had been pre-empted by a Japanese brand. Not overly familiar with recent U.S. advertising, I had assumed that this was a purely locally developed campaign, particularly as the company responsible was very Japanese in character. Since my U.S. client assured me that the similarity of the advertising concept could not have been due to a coincidence, obviously this Japanese company was not too hung-up on the fact that "the Japanese are different."

Too often the "Japan is different" council is given with an axe to grind—to enhance the local position and make the helpless foreigners depend on local advice—be it Japanese or resident foreigners. You can make a better judgment on this advice if your starting point is your product—its raison d'être in the market—and *not* your advertising, which seems obvious but is a rule that is not always adhered to.

The "Japan is Becoming Westernized" Syndrome

Our Japanese colleagues are as confused on this matter as we are. On the one hand, Japan and the Japanese are unique, while, on the other hand, they belong more to the Western camp, it is said, than to the East. In the 1960s, many of my Japanese colleagues delighted in quoting Professor Edwin Reischauer that Japan should be called the "Far West" rather than the "Far East." The visible "Westernization" is one of the most dangerous traps you can fall into initially when you are considering your advertising strategy, because it does not follow from this that your marketing strategy, let alone your advertising, developed in the home market will work. If it happens to work, it is not because the Japanese are getting Westernized; it is probably because there is a coherent principle or a benefit that is shared.

The habit of perceiving Westernization in non-Western cultures probably has its origin in the Industrial Revolution, and what is really meant, in many cases, is "modernization." For roughly the past 150 years, Westernization was synonymous with modernization, which has led to a degree of cultural arrogance on the part of the Westerner and a tendency to oversimplify in this respect. Eating a Big Mac doesn't make a Tokyoite Westernized; nor does eating sushi Japanize a New Yorker. In considering a strategy for your product, it is best to remind yourself that a product will be consumed, not because it is Western or Japanese, but because it can be positioned in the consumer's life, which is constantly evolving.

Whisky consumption is just as prevelant as that of saké consumption, and nobody even thinks of the No. 1 one alcoholic beverage, beer, as a Western-origin product. There is a historical, cultural reason why these three account for 90% of alcoholic-beverage consumption in Japan. White liquors such as rum and vodka have become No. 1 brands in the U.S., gin and sherry have been traditionally popular in Britain, and champagne does well in France; in comparison, consumption of these liquors is miniscule in Japan. Now, the trend may eventually be toward white liquor or diversification into a host of other drinks as in the United States, but if it happens, the reasons for it are likely to be different. Until recently, there was no evidence that this would happen, but the decline in whisky consumption has forced Suntory, the major maker, into campaigns to expand into other alcoholic beverages. Range expansion will occur not because it happened in the U.S. but only if successful positionings can be found in the Japanese consumers' drinking life.

In the 1960s, Western-style soup found itself, unexpectedly to some, on the Japanese breakfast table, whereas it has been a long haul for breakfast cereals, which are only now making a breakthrough. It was easier for soup to be served for the Japanese breakfast than cereal, because, traditionally, Japanese bean-paste soup (*misoshiru*) was always served for breakfast; thus, when the breakfast started to turn Western, with toast and margarine, etc., Western-style soup had no conceptual problems being positioned. In a traditionally salt-oriented Japanese breakfast, cereals with milk and sugar had problems in this respect, with the more traditionally minded older generation. However, the new generation of youngsters is changing in this respect. The boom on home baking of bread for breakfast in 1987, cited earlier, has a solid cultural base. The Japanese housewives traditionally served hot rice for breakfast and freshly baked bread is a natural extension. It really has nothing to do with her becoming "Westernized" in substituting bread for rice. In fact, how many Western housewives these days yearn for freshly baked bread in the morning?

Concept and Positioning

Advertising as a discipline in the West has not always followed scientific methods or moved along logical lines, although once it became an industry, adoption of these were inevitable. The process in which we develop hypotheses (or concepts), test them, and finally execute them inevitably follows Western intellectual processes. It is not surprising that the word "concept," which we so freely use, when rendered into Japanese becomes *gainen*, a somewhat esoteric term in philosophy. In the context of free-wheeling brainstorming sessions, the word *gainen* just doesn't fit, so if used at all, it is now *konseputo* (in *katakana*, the Japanese phonetic alphabet, of course).

In entering the Japanese market and in planning your advertising strategy, this Western-derived discipline of examining your product or advertising concept in the Japanese context is your essential first step. Most of the techniques developed by the Western advertising and market research fraternity are available here and applied with equal zest by the Japanese advertising industry—despite the "Japan is different" syndrome; here you are in familiar territory and I am not aware of purely endogenous techniques, although this is not to say that emphasis does not vary and that modifications are not made. I believe that the information you require at this stage must be qualitative as well as quantiative.

The "Most Japanese Advertising is Mood" Syndrome

It is as patently absurd to assert that most Japanese advertising is based on "mood" as it is to say that most American advertising is based on "logic," and yet it continues to be made—one thing I always found unchanged in my first 20 odd years of work in Japan. With the ascension of the Japanese corporation in world business, all of a sudden, the critics of Japanese advertising have diminished in number. Early reactions were often emotionally charged with the underlying frustration that one's principles were being betrayed. As a market researcher, I should have shared this frustration, since "mood" is hard to define and hence hard to measure. Some had fallen into the trap of simply defining good advertising as that which can be measured by some defined criteria. If this is not the tail wagging the dog, I would like to know what is.

Common sense tells us that advertising is not independent of the culture and that otherwise astute Japanese businessmen would not consider squandering money on efforts that did not yield returns. When we watch television, we all make judgments on "good" and "bad" commercials, and of course the more empirical data we have, the more comfortable we are in making these judgments. I submit that in any country, if we have the TV turned on all day, we would conclude, judgmentally, that there seem to be more "poor" commercials than "good" ones; that is because we tend to consider the "average" commercial as "poor" and since, by definition, there are fewer "above average" ones, it then follows that there are fewer "good" commercials.

In one's own culture, it is easier to perceive an "intuitive average." What happens when the foreigner comes to Japan is that the "average"—or more correctly the "mode"—deviates a lot more from his own or from that of most other cultures with which he is familiar.

I can show many examples of "successful" Japanese advertising that are not based on "mood." Equally, there are many that can be considered "mood" and typically Japanese. This does not prove anything, because I could produce an equal batch for *both* that were not successful. Just the same as in the U.S. or anywhere, there is simply no absolute rule for good advertising. Do not be deceived by "the mood is more important" claim. What should be recognized is that the "cultural mode" is different from your own and that you may have to formulate and judge your advertising perhaps differently from how you normally would. The "mood" versus "logic" issue can be a red herring and is reexamined later.

International Comparisons

If your strategy was successful in many other countries—and "those countries all claimed that they were different" — you have a major jump on your competition in that you have advertising vehicles that can be tested. On the other hand, while the fact that it was successful in several other countries may increase your confidence and make you feel that your probability of success is greater, it is largely irrelevant to the issue. "Western" logical training should tell you that this just does not follow and that you should take the same precautions as when you first launched the product. This has another advantage in that comparison of data will immediately enable you to spot any differences. The fact that you have a track record elsewhere is clearly an advantage but if it leads to over-confidence, it is a disadvantage.

There is probably more misunderstanding on both sides—among Japanese and the Western marketers—when it comes to comparing reaction, performances, or other kinds of data with facts obtained elsewhere. Disregarding the "Japan is different" syndrome, the reactions of your Japanese colleagues—that overseas research criteria are inapplicable—are sometimes justified, although the objections are often not well articulated.

John Cobbs in a *Business Week* article (Nov. 19, 1979) remarked that "the U.S. obsession with statistics is so deeply rooted that it takes an occasional error to remind the users that some figures might as well be pulled out of a hat." He also gave the well-known quotation from M.J. Moroney's *Facts from Figures:* "There is more than a germ of truth in the suggestion that, in a society where statisticians thrive, liberty and individuality are likely to be emasculated. Historically, statistics is no more than State Arithmetic, a system of computation by which differences between individuals are eliminated by the taking of an average."

To many Japanese, Westerners are indeed over-dependent on statistics. It is not an entirely Japanese phenomenon for creative people to object to the use of figures, because it stifles their imaginative freedom and puts them into a straitjacket of averages; worse still, if the figures are derived elsewhere. You will have a hard time convincing your Japanese colleagues that your overseas norms are applicable here, and as far as advertising is concerned, I contend that they are perhaps more often right than not. It is a little like Einstein's world, in that although you may be applying the same yardsticks, depending on the circumstances, they may be longer or shorter. One advantage of operating interculturally is that we are able to pinpoint some of the differences and in some cases come to a controversial conclusion that *the same technique may be generating a different measure*. The measures themselves are equally valid, but applying the *same* interpretations may have dire consequences by being misleading.

So you have at least two issues to contend with when you make international comparisons: (1) Can overseas data be used as benchmarks? and (2) Does the data represent the same measurements?

On behavioral data such as that on the percentage of homes owning a household appliance, there are no problems. However, if you relied on a rating scale to decide on whether a concept will fly, you may be in trouble. Early in my career in Japan, I was involved in a project in which over thirty concepts were to be screened, using the same techniques that were used in the United States, the United Kingdom, Germany, and Australia. In each case, the most critical measure was a "top-of-the-box" rating on a certain scale. On this basis, all concepts failed in Japan, but worse still, the data were nondiscriminating, that is, the figures were similar for all concepts.

I hasten to add that the client was warned of this possibility, but of course the experience of all the other countries could not be ignored, and it was the client's prerogative to decide that the exercise be conducted. The data was discriminating to some extent when the top two boxes were combined, but this raised a quandary in that one could not be sure whether the discrimination simply indicated differences between mediocrities—some are not as bad as others—or the superiority of some over others. In any event, persistence on norms derived from the other four countries proved to be a clear case of the tail wagging the dog.

Known Measurement Differences

I do not have an exhaustive list of measurement differences, and it seems that we in the profession should bury our competitive hatchets and get together and pool our knowledge. The instance cited above, however, will be a common experience to all market researchers operating inter-culturally in Japan. The scaling effect, as we call it, does illustrate a fascinating cultural phenomena, and when I describe it to my Japanese colleagues, they seem to find that it makes sense. The "theory" simply stated is that when confronted with a verbal 7-point scale or whatever, say ranging from "excellent" to "terrible," Westerners tend to start from the extremes, that is, to consider a position quickly and then perhaps to modify it, which means working from both ends and moving toward the center. The Japanese, on the other hand, tend to take a neutral position or start from the mid-point and move outwards, seldom reaching the extremes, hence the low "top of the box" ratings. Using even number scales, or those without a strict mid-point, doesn't really resolve the issue. While this explanation is a little pat, it fits our usual observations of the Japanese being very cautious to take up a fixed position, before all known facts and consequences are weighed. How then can one give a clear opinion on a product or an advertisement in a single-shot or short-term exposure? Here, *time* is the substance rather than the number of exposures.

Another discovery that we stumbled upon—simply because we were fortunate in having access to data generated from identical laboratory-controlled procedures—was that there are specific differences in verbal versus non-verbal sensitivities. Since discussion of these will take us away from our subject, and since it has been published elsewhere, I will give only the basic proposition. The

Westerner has a greater ability to comprehend aural messages than the Japanese and to transmit them verbally: the Japanese have a greater capacity to respond to visual stimuli and to interpret them symbolically. Now we are getting closer to the core than with the "mood" versus "logic" argument.

The point here is that measurements on various advertising criteria are not absolutes and must be evaluated in relation to the cultural environment. It may so happen that they are identical to your previous experiences—but what if they are not? Clearly, norms that have been developed within the culture must be applied.

Concept Versus Execution: A Matter of Style

Fifteen or so years ago, I would have queried this subheading, for the two are not in conflict. My training in a multinational corporation's marketing school told me that the concept comes first and then the execution. The concept had to be right, for you can always improve the execution; however, if the concept was not right, then an excellent execution would not save the situation. I still agree with this basic tenet, but for a while I had my doubts after a few years in Japan. The doubts have been dispelled, for me at least, in realizing that "style" was not necessarily a matter of execution but could also be part of the concept!

It does not take very long for one to realize the importance of form in Japan; as a manager, despite my Japanese childhood background, I have more than once had to rue the fact that it was not the decision that I made *per se* that some of my staff objected to, but it was the way I made it. A Western colleague put it another way—"it's not what you say but how you say it." On this, Americans and

Australians in particular tend to be derogatory, with remarks such as "form over substance." Still, this is really a value judgment, and, while it may make an interesting debate topic, the pros and cons are irrelevant in this context. However, it may be noted that it is the newer cultures, such as those of the United States and Australia, that are different from the rest in this respect, and it is not a question of which is right or wrong.

Examples of the importance of form (or style) abound. As noted in another section, the department stores in Japan have a lion's share of the huge gift market: the same box of soap is acceptable in a Takashimaya department store wrapping but may not have nearly the same value, in the receiver's eyes, if it comes from the local supermarket. Even the British, who would normally be regarded as being more respectful of form and style than many, are radicals compared with the Japanese. What is said by the actors in a Shakespearean production is of vital importance even to the novice playgoer. However, for the average Kabuki goer, the pleasure is in seeing the stylistic flourishes handed down within the great Kabuki families, and, more often than not, how the dialogue is delivered generates more enthusiasm than the understanding of what is said. (Mind you, this could also be true of a line delivered by a great Shakespearean actor, so it is still a matter of emphasis.) The Japanese *itamae*—rough equivalent of the Western chef—is applauded for the visual pleasure his preparation gives, for the way it is presented, and for his attention to even minor details.

The Japanese are faced with intricate sets of dos and don'ts in their daily living—in speech and in manner of conduct; all cultures have them, but the insistence toward formalities is certainly far greater than in the United States or even in most European cultures. It would be naive to expect that advertising alone would be exempted from some of these rules. The Japanese advertisers have found ways to get around them—some of them perplexing to the Western advertiser. It is my theory that many of the slapstick presentations are rough equivalents to the straight stand-up pitch in the United States. In a culture in which modesty is still one of the prime virtues—"the riper the rice, the deeper it bows its head"—some straight pitches are considered "too pushy." However, a pair of slapstick comedians can put the point across very effectively—since they are making idiots of themselves, they are not offensive and yet the point they have made has sunk in. The Westerner's reaction to this patently nonsensical behavior could be that it downgrades the "seriousness" of the product and cheapens it in the eyes of the consumer.

The above course is, however, dangerous for the foreigner to take and probably precluded, because humor of this kind tends to be peculiar to the culture, rather than universal. If getting around the rules is not advisable, then one is forced into abiding by them, and this seems to be quite often ignored by the "straight transfer" school. It is true that some great campaigns have been developed by "breaking the rules" and that there is the contention that it is "better to offend than not to be noticed." However, the price of social offense varies by place and circumstances, and one must not be reckless in this respect. As consumer response is fairly easy to check, you should at least make sure that the "offense" causes you to be noticed and *not* mentally blocked out. I know of numerous cases in which a seemingly minor detail to a Westerner caused the latter to happen.

It was David Ogilvy who said that advertising should provide the consumer with a "first-class ticket" to the product, or a "green car" ticket, in the case of Japan. A cheap, shoddily executed commercial creates a subconscious impression in the viewer that the product is also so. A commercial that goes against perceived good taste and accepted style within the culture may make the Japanese consumer feel that the product does not belong in his or her daily life and is for the oddball.

Returning then to the subheading of this section, "Concept Versus Execution," do not be surprised when your Japanese creative man presents you with a storyboard that seems to be based on an "executional" idea rather than a firm concept. What confuses both as an executional element may represent an important idea stylistically presented like the Kabuki actor's frozen stance, which may symbolically position your product. It is not essential that a concept be capable of verbalization.

Verbal Versus Nonverbal Communication

Here I am not referring to "body language," a popular psychosocial concern of the recent past. It has some relationship to aural versus visual communication, although not entirely. In the current context, as already implied, it has great relevance to the perception of advertising in terms of "logical" versus "mood" presentation.

Our discovery in this respect was touched upon above ("Known Measurement Differences"). Recent works have shown that the communication tools themselves encourage unique developments in the Japanese ability to perceive.

An interesting clue to this phenomena emerged incidentally in a medical case study. In the 1960s, a young doctor at the Kobe University Hospital, Dr. Atsushi Yamadori, published an unusual thesis proposing that "the ideographic characters of *kanji* (Chinese characters) and phonetic symbols of *kana* were memorized in different parts of the brain.'' The actual title of the paper was "The Reading of Chinese Characters in Alexia,'' and was a case report on one of his patients, who had been hospitalized after cerebral apoplexy. Incredibly, as an aftereffect, this patient had completely forgotten *katakana* and *hiragana*, both Japanese-developed phonetic symbols, as opposed to the Chinese ideographs, which he retained his ability to read. Since the Japanese communicate by using both methods of writing, it meant that he could no longer read the newspaper as the phonetic portion was blocked out. He could write his name and address, which were all in *kanji*, but not sentences. As such a "pure case" was rare, checks were repeated over two years before the conclusion was reached that "unlike phonetic symbols, which were stored in the left sphere of the brain, *kanji* were stored in the right sphere, like pictures.'' Our own data, taken together with this finding, suggests that the Japanese ability to perceive symbols is greater than that of the Westerner, perhaps due to the long conditioning he receives in learning *kanji*. The Oriental art of calligraphy is far removed from penmanship in the West.

The Western foundation of "intellectual" communication could be said to have been established by the Greeks and is essentially a culture of "debate.'' The Western businessman states his position at a meeting—the thesis—and this is probably taken up by a counter point of view—the antithesis. After further debate, the meeting is expected to arrive at some sort of decision and resolution—the synthesis. It is essentially an aural system of communication.

The Japanese, on the other hand, have no such tradition of verbal debate. Jack Seward, in his very perceptive book, *Japanese In Action* (purportedly for students in semantics), gives a very vivid illustration. In the highly structured Japanese society of the samurai, the farmer, the artisan, and the merchant—in that order of social ranking—free and direct verbal communication could be quite risky. The samurai had absolute rights over the rest of the community, described as *kirisute gomen*, literally, "I can chop your head off and you have no recourse to the courts." The samurai, on the whole, did not abuse this right, in order to avoid the social upheaval that would result from total oppression. The fact remains that such a right existed, and thus there emerged a very cautious form of verbal response within the community generally. Obviously, one should not offend by giving the wrong answer. But it came about that if you could not be certain of the right answer, it was better for everybody if you answered in a way that could be interpreted as either "yes" or "no."

In modern-day Japan, such an illustration may seem exaggerated. Certainly, the legacy of the Tokugawa samurai era is fading, although it still remains to a large extent in the administrative infrastructure of the government and of many of the larger corporations. The point is, however, that given these very different historical backgrounds to the process of communication, the way in which an advertising message may be conveyed even in present-day Japan, may be, and in many cases is, quite different from that in Western cultures.

Earlier I warned of the "Japan is different syndrome" and the "all commercials are mood" syndrome, so now it may seem that I am contradicting my earlier position. I would put it to the reader that the importance of having the "right" concept and "effective" positioning is no different between the cultures. I am, however, contending that differences in execution are inevitable—especially in the matter of style and in emphasis. As for "mood," some commercials that you consider to be "mood" have proved to be effective, while others not. Their success and failure really had little to do with whether they were "mood" commercials or not. When we examine "mood" commercials that are successful, we find that they contain an idea that is visually or symbolically presented and perhaps only noticed and understood by those within the culture. Lack of verbal content does not necessarily mean an absence of an advertising concept. On the other hand, those that failed probably did so for the same reason that some non-mood commercials fail—because of the lack of a meaningful concept or of improper positioning of the product.

In planning his advertising strategy, the Western professional need not feel that his expertise is inapplicable to Japan. I believe that he can contribute very effectively in the systematic development and examination of concepts. On the other hand, he should not dismiss out of hand or be scornful of objections raised by his local colleagues, even if they don't quite fit his conception of logic. In the matter of concept and execution, the ultimate judge is, after all, the Japanese consumer.

PART FOUR

CONSUMERS ARISE, YOUR DAY IS NEAR

THE HITHERTO SILENT JAPANESE CONSUMERS

Not Attacking the Fundamentals

OLD JAPAN HANDS eventually stop noticing cultural differences. That may also be why the Japanese are not generally good at explaining themselves to the West. Fortunately, due to the nature of my job, I am continuously exposed to perceptive observations by newcomers. This time, though, I noticed something even without their help.

The scene on my TV screen one evening in 1986 was pretty boring. For a non-Japanese-speaking foreigner, it could have passed as a high-school graduation ceremony except that the students would have been handing the certificates back to their teacher and they were all much older than the teacher. One by one they filed by, presented a document, bowed, and stepped back. Incredible as it may have seemed to some foreigners, these were heads of power companies presenting a senior MITI official with notifications of new lower rates to the consumer.

Of course, this was triggered by the sudden rise in the yen. As a consumer, I was not particularly impressed that the reduction was based on ¥178 rather than the then rate of ¥160. The net savings on energy costs for an average family in the Tokyo area was around ¥1,500 a month, but at least it was a start. Still, I was tremendously impressed at the lightning speed in which the deed was effected. I remember that rates for overseas phone calls were held at ¥320 to the dollar for years, over a period when the going rate drifted to around ¥200, and nobody thought of reducing prices then.

But even at the new pricing, energy still costs considerably more than in the United States and most Western countries. Isn't there somebody on the consumer side that is concerned about higher prices? If I could banish one phrase from the consumer vocabulary, it would be *Shikata ga nai*, or, "So what can a small fry like me do?" That's the point—the individual consumer in Japan is helpless and has no spokesperson on this issue.

Quite a few market change predictions in the past have not materialized because they assumed consumer sovereignty. One concerned the notorious distribution system, adversely affecting the free flow of products from the rest of the world. Its inefficiency—half the population of the United States but the same number employed in the industry, which simply translates as only half the efficiency—contributes mightily to the high cost of products. So with the advent of the supermarket, it was thought that the number of small retail outlets would be reduced since they cannot possibly compete in price. But in stepped the government to pass laws to inhibit the growth of supermarkets and to prolong the agony of high prices. I am not aware of vociferous protests by consumer groups on this score, at the time. With admirable humanistic instincts, their sympathies were with the little guy who will be driven out by the more efficient big baddies.

However, there is virtual silence when the biggies blatantly fix prices. In early 1986, I sat on a panel that included a housewife as a representative of a consumer group. The audience was composed of overseas businessmen brought over for the occasion, and somehow the panel was supposed to help them learn how to sell more to Japan. A better understanding of the Japanese culture was one way. Greater simplification of import procedures was another. I naturally assumed that our consumer representative would be all for imports that would reduce the price pressure on her constituency. The audience was first lectured on the high standards set by the Japanese consumer on product quality, not always met by imports. True enough. Then too, she said, Japan has the world's highest safety standards for such things as toys, appliances, and food. "We certainly cannot jeopardize the safety of our kids."

My mouth gaped when she declared that trade liberalization implied the lowering of safety standards and she would prefer higher prices to that. In 1988, this was the main thrust to the movement to prevent liberalization of foreign farm products. Many Japanese consumers are genuinely concerned that theirs and their children's health will be jeoparadized by imports. But back to the 1986 panel. It was now my turn. "Well, I understand that there are almost a quarter of million Japanese stationed abroad now. Almost 5 million travel overseas yearly. If the Western countries have such lax safety standards, how come we never hear of mass food poisonings and electrocutions? Or is it that in some mysterious ways, these goods become dangerous when they hit the Japanese shores?" I knew I had departed from my expected role of explaining the inscrutable Japanese consumer. I was now the puzzled one at the lack of true consumer representation on the price issue.

We are told continuously of the bottom-up Japanese-style of

management and how superior it is to the top-down Western type. As far as the Japanese consumer is concerned, the direction has always been top-down. It is about time that they, rather than the producers, receive the fruits of industrial productivity and diligence. The burden of the minority, who are less efficient, should not be shouldered by the consumer as a whole. They deserve to benefit from the pressure for internationalization and not suffer because of it.

When are the Japanese consumer groups going to start complaining about institutional price fixing, whether it be for air fares, beef, postage or telephone rates, books, etc., etc., that keeps many products more expensive than in other advanced economies with no trade surplus to show? Japanese consumer advocates, where are you?

Let Us Consumers Buy What We Want

If stimulation of domestic demand and a reduction in the saving rate are what Japan needs, why not cut out the government as middleman and let the people decide what to buy? This, of course, is the consistent editorial position maintained by a number of news publications these days, whether applied to other countries or the United States. With the current consensus that Japan should "internationalize," the proposition seems eminently reasonable.

However, when examining trends, there is a tendency to be carried away with the conspicuous, too often overlooking the counterforce to change. Whenever Japan's *shinjinrui* (new generation) is discussed, we tend to exaggerate their impact on societal values, overlooking the formidable conventional forces aligned against them, such as those, for example, they face when they enter a corporation or get married. While it is often assumed that removal of official interference is enough to free the consumer, it isn't as simple as that. There is also the assumption that the Japanese consumer, like his counterpart in the U.S., is guided by grass roots principles. He isn't.

May 30 has been designated as "Consumers' Day," and ironically, two authoritative non-government sources have already come out with warnings against unfettered imports of foreign products. True to form, one is Japan's Consumer Union. In a pamphlet, only one out of a spate of recent publications on the subject, the consumer is warned of the danger of imports. We are not talking about AIDS, but rice. The pamphlet is entitled "Importing rice? You must be kidding!"

We are all familiar with the self-sufficiency argument—propagated by the farm lobby—that Japan cannot be totally reliant on imports for essential foodstuffs. The previous crisis over soybeans is cited, when exports were temporarily suspended during the Nixon administration. But the warning is repeated — and it has been Japan's official stance — that imported foodstuffs may be dangerous. Claims are that imports contain unacceptable levels of preservatives, insecticides and herbicides. One can respond by pointing out that Japan itself is a major market for insecticides and herbicides. As for preservatives, there are strict rules that prevent imports that do not meet clearly specified standards; the consumer is already protected and does not need to be warned about it. The vast number of Japanese travelers to Southeast Asia and the United States seem unconcened about eating the rice of other nations during their sojourns, and if this rice is as dangerous as the Consumer Union suggests, these travelers should be warned before going abroad.

It is also said that "blind" taste tests indicate the inferiority of the foreign product. This argument reminds me of a famous soft-drink campaign. But that was fought in the open market-place and the comsumer was not prevented from trying the "inferior" product. Consumers, by the way, are known to accept trade-offs on quality when given a substantial reduction in price—say one-sixth of the total retail price. So why not just come clean and say that Japanese consumers don't like the idea of eating foreign rice and be done with it? It is more honest to admit to consumer nationalism than to continuously bring out red herrings that can be refuted. If no one in Japan wants to eat foreign rice, under free conditions, then there will be no imports and the fuss will die down.

Objections from other authoritative sources take a somewhat different view, although one is still concerned with the safety issue. Michiko Kamiyama, representing the "Environmental Pollution and Consumer Issues Special Subcommittee" of the Japan Bar Association, takes up the cudgel in the *Asahi Shimbun*. She cites the fairly recent harm inflicted on consumers through asphyxiation from fan heaters (which are local products) and wine, such as the Austrian scandal caused by the use of diethylene glycol as a sweetening agent. By raising the issue as a matter of urgency relative to the current trend toward internationalization, she subtly implies that imports can be a source of danger.

Ms. Kamiyama, however, has a valid point when she says that the lack of open information for the consumer must be corrected. In the U.S., there are public forums for challenge, and these are open to any consumer, not just to self-appointed representatives. In the "Basic Acts for the Protection of the Consumer" issued in Japan in 1968, the term "consumer's rights" is absent. Ms. Kamiyama says that if the government is to succumb to the pressures of internationalization by relaxing its regulations and reducing its participation in consumer protection, then it must tackle the issue of free access to product information and the right to challenge. This is fine, except that it will create further procrastination and delay while officials, perhaps including those of the Bar Association, haggle over the new rules. Unfortunately, it will only remind the world that Japan is awfully good at coming up with reasons for postponing access to its market and that Japanese officials have once again come up with a new tactic.

Nobody expects Japan to withdraw to the *sakoku* (total isolation) policies practiced during the Tokugawa shogunate. Its only real alternative today is to remove restrictions on the consumer's freedom to buy or not to buy. This departure from consumer nationalism will continue, despite the efforts of forces trying to prevent it. All they can really do is to delay it.

It can never be as simple as recent editorials suggest, but the self-appointed official protectors of the Japanese consumer have less time than they think. The battle over consumer liberation is headed toward a rapid showdown.

Mom, Mt. Fuji, and Rice

The debate on a recent Sunday night television program was an unusual spectacle. It was most un-Japanese in that members of the audience clamored to be heard and, more strikingly, vehemently contradicted some of the eminent panel members. Panel members, too, disagreed with one another. The controversial subject was the liberalization of the Japanese market for farm products.

Significantly, the debate focused on beef and oranges—categories on which the U.S. is taking its case to GATT (General Agreement on Tariffs and Trade)—and rice was more or less left out. Of the token foreigners in the audience, the only one queried quite understandably ducked the issue, since it is clearly a serious domestic

matter. The debate was a reminder to me that with all the concentration on change by numerous commentators—East and West, and
yours truly included—basic values do not change overnight.

Only a few days before this, I had been asked on a U.S. television
program why the Japanese are so stubborn on the issue of farm products. The U.S. view seems to be that it is a political problem caused
by the ruling Liberal-Democratic Party's dependence on the farm
vote. That is true as far as the LDP is concerned, but the consumer
has another perspective which clearly distinguishes beef and oranges
from rice. Their views deserve consideration.

It is essential for the U.S. to understand that the majority of
Japanese consumers oppose the importation of rice, even if it brings
the price down. Feelings are not so strong for beef and oranges and
the reasons for this go well beyond politics.

From the time of first recorded history—and in Japan the birth of
literature goes back to the last part of the sixth century—Japan was
not only a rice economy but a rice culture. The rice paddy was an efficient means of providing sustenance in preindustrial Japan and was
eminently attuned to Japanese nature. The resulting reservoir of
subterranean water contributed to the lush greenery of the coun-
tryside. Thus, the highly dependent sense of harmony that ensued
owes a great deal to this means of sustenance. In the *waka*
poems—from the earliest collections of the *Kokinshu*—the change of
the four seasons is noted as the most significant binding thread, as the
growing and harvesting of rice through the seasons was an important
ritual. Under the Tokugawa shogunate, for example, the rank of a
samurai was designated, among other considerations, by the number
of bushels of rice he received from his daimyo in lieu of a salary.

Industrialization, which ultimately transformed the nation into a
foremost economic power, also posed a dilemma in the destruction of

nature. Arguments have been advanced that the preservation of the rice economy has saved Japan from total pollution. The government, the farm lobby, and the media have been successful in painting a picture of desolation—in the form of total disappearance of the rice paddy from the Japanese landscape—if imports are liberalized. Only a minority of informed specialists argue that the more efficient will survive by producing rice of perceived merit to the consumer, thus justifying its higher price.

A Japanese landscape without any rice paddies, already destroyed to a large extent by factories and unsightly urban sprawl, does not bear contemplation by residents of these crowded islands. So the Japanese are not being totally selfish, as is the usual perception by the rest of the world.

The U.S. also experienced a similar emotional crisis concerning its farmland. A number of movies depicted embattled farm families struggling against formidable odds, and Bruce Springsteen appealed emotionally through song to urban audiences. Can we imagine the U.S. without those vast "amber waves of grain"? Of course not. If this is so for the North American continent, why should it not generate even more intense feelings in the small and congested islands of Japan?

The Japanese appear unable to convey the emotional argument to the United States—there is no place for such appeal in hard-nosed negotiations on trade issues. It would probably be brushed aside as just another excuse, anyway. But an important point is being missed: It is not a question of economics, but of the perceived disappearance of a distinct cultural foundation.

The Japanese themselves make a mistake in obscuring the issue by resting their case on self-sufficiency and the highly insulting suggestion that they are the only ones competent in controlling safety. Obviously, Japanese rice production would not survive if importation of herbicides suddenly ceased, and, as was proved during World War II, rice alone will not sustain them for very long.

The U.S. is justified in pressing for reforms that will remove institutional rigidity to facilitate freer movement of goods. The television debate showed that the message had gotten through. The U.S. pressure is benefiting the Japanese consumer's stance, and the push for the removal of political protection has begun. This point is reflected in a poll conducted by the *Asahi Shimbun* during March 1988: while 55% of the respondents opposed the importation of rice, 70% felt that current controls kept prices unnecessarily high. Although it may seem that there is a substantial minority in favor of importation, a further 12% felt that imports will bring down the price of Japanese rice, so some 70% are in favor of continued rice production in Japan.

Since the U.S. is a populist culture, it should respect the feelings of the Japanese majority rather than simply dismiss consumer predilection as a result of official brainwashing. The U.S. is committing a grave error in lumping all farm products together at the expense of true consumer sentiment. The relationship of the two countries is far too important for the U.S. to ride roughshod over Japan's grassroots emotions. In terms of consumer values and cultural attitudes, beef and oranges are well removed from the rice issue.

A Funny Thing Happened on the Way to the Airport

With all the long-term market watching that I have been doing in Japan I should not have been surprised by a certain intrusion of the FTC (Fair Trade Commission) into the market place and the fact that its attitude stanchly remains the same, although times are said to have changed. The FTC still seems worried about "competitive chaos," termed *katō kyōsō*, and its paramount mission is to protect society from this hazard. New entrants are always suspect in this regard, since they have a peculiar penchant for disturbing cozy arrangements among the market incumbents.

Without the FTC watching over me, I as a consumer, would be easy prey for peace-disturbing enticements. For example, an airline was offering a free door-to-door limousine service from my home in Tokyo to Narita Airport, then from the airport at the destination to my hotel. But then I found from the newspaper that the airline was being very naughty and that it had been hauled over the coals by the FTC for this action. It appeared that the airline had infringed upon a rule called "the prevention of unjust premiums and unjust indications." As a matter of fact, this rule happens to be a longstanding bone of contention with foreign consumer marketers. For products or services, any premiums offered must not exceed 10% of the value with the absolute maximum, irrespective of the price, at ¥50,000. It was claimed that the limousine fares to and from the airports exceeded this maximum, even for first-class fares. The airline was already providing this service on its Atlantic routes, where it had not been suggested as a means of "unfair" competition. But here we go again—Japan is different.

The FTC says that marketers should compete "fairly" on quality and that excessive premiums are harmful because they distract the consumer from "fair" evaluations of the products or services. It also argues that premium offers give large marketers, with strength and financial reserves, "unfair" advantages over the small. Unfortunately, as applied in Japan, this reminds me of Anatole France's dictum, which I think went something like this: "The law is perfectly fair; it prohibits both the rich and the poor from sleeping under the bridge.''

In many cases, the newcomer is the smaller company who is prepared to take the gamble of introducing his product or service by cutting his margins to accelerate consumer trial. In a famous instance, a U.S. marketer, renowned for his skill in premium marketing in his own country, was prevented from using this method when he entered the Japanese market. The joke was that the market was dominated by two Japanese giants who were unlikely to be run out of town by the newcomer. In any case, according to the FTC's logic, the two Japanese giants had greater reserves to ''unfairly'' retaliate. Did the FTC seriously think that Japan's national airline was in jeopardy because of the limousine transfer offer? Anyway, so what? Let the better service prevail irrespective of whether it is on the ground or on board. The hypocrisy of it is that, outside of Japan, Japanese marketers are known for being disturbers of market status quo through their willingness to cut margins to capture market share, and I have defended it as a legitimate long-term strategy.

As a consumer, I have a naive wish. For a change, I wish the FTC would allow me to benefit from competition and leave it to the people in the Ministry of Health and the police to protect me from danger. For example, why is it that it is more economical for me to buy a one-way ticket for London in Tokyo and buy my return in London, rather than buying a round-trip ticket in Japan? Why is it that I cannot qualify for a frequent traveler program as a resident in Japan, while the same airline grants the privilege to my friends who live overseas? Why is that it costs my daughter less to phone me from the United States than for me to call her? Why do I only get the benefits of a strong yen when I'm out of the counry? But listing all the questions I have accumulated over the years would only result in a monotonous litany. Not all of them come under the FTC's jurisdiction, but giving priority to preserving stability in the market, favors cartels rather than consumers and naturally results in higher prices.

A Matter of Social Conscience or Official Governance

There is a saying common to both English and Japanese. In Japanese it's *doronawa,* which means making a rope to catch a thief after a burglary; in English, it is locking the barn after the horse has bolted. Both suggest that action after an event is futile. But in many cases, extra precautions after the fact do ensure that it won't happen again. So moves to ensure that illegal marketing—as in the Toshiba COCOM incident—never happens again make certain sense.

But the similarity of the two sayings notwithstanding, there seems to be a substantial perception gap concerning the Toshiba incident between Japan and the United States. At the private level, much of the debate in Japan at the time was not meant for U.S. consumption. However, as with the earlier controvesial Nakasone remark on the superiority of a homogeneous society, information thse days moves quickly. One effect of internationalization is that there are more foreigners who understand Japanese!

A distinguished Japanese speaker declared at a recent top management· seminar that a U.S. defense-related magazine had published an article at least twelve months before the Toshiba Machine Tool Co.'s breach of the COCOM agreement that diminution of the sound level from the screws of Russian submarines had been detected. He went on to say that Japan should stand up to such "Japan bashing," a phrase invented by the American press but now taken into the Japanese vernacular. He is not alone in this view. But this strikes me as a peculiar *doronawa* argument. The fact that the Russians already had access to the equipment is morally irrelevant. It's rather like saying, "I gave a thief the key to your house, but don't worry, you had already been robbed."

The early position taken by the Keidanren (Federation of Economic Organizations) was that it involved malpractice by an individual company and, thus, there was no need for all of Japan to go into an act of contrition. This is a logical attitude, and I see nothing wrong with it. Americans would have said the same. But matters got complicated when Toshiba executives resigned over an act committed by a separate company over which they had no jurisdiction, seemingly acknowledging culpability. (Would an American executive have resigned?) The problem was still Toshiba's.

The initial complacency was also due to the fact that the matter supposedly concerned defense and not trade in general—again, a logical position that could and should have been argued strongly. Then, as passions started to flare, and with the threat that more pockets would be affectd, there was a change in position to support the actions of the government in amending the "Foreign Exchange and Foreign Trade Control Act" that deals strongly with infringements. On the surface, that seems fair enough, but coming rather late in the day, a cynic would suggest that it was an empty gesture, not one from the heart, to placate the Americans.

For a foreign firm doing business in Japan for any length of time, that particular law brings a shudder. It has been used very effectively in the past to control the free workings of the market. Early on in our business, we had a cash shortage; being foreign and too new, we were precluded from an adequate local line of credit. In my naivete I thought that, unlike sending yen out, bringing dollars in would be welcomed. However, if we had not had a cash-rich sister company operating in Japan, we could have been in trouble, since the bureaucratic procedures of remitting money from the head office were extremely time consuming and came under the above law.

Japanese legal experts are now concerned that under the revised act, the loose definition of infringement, tied to the maintenance of peace and security in general, gives officials carte blanche to restrict trade. Given Japanese officialdom's past record, the fear that the new act will further complicate foreign exchange procedures seems justified. If the community takes the view that private business cannot be trusted—an attitude held in socialist economies—then restrictions are inevitable. The business community's enthusiastic endorsement of open-ended bureaucratic powers of restrictions in this instance is tantamount to passing the buck. I hope the cure is not going to be worse than the symptom.

The Japanese Consumer Wise or Stupid?

I frequently quote the late American humorist Robert Benchley as saying, "There are two types of people. Those who classify people into two types and those who don't." One type of society works on the premise that human nature is essentially good, while the other side takes the opposite view. Capitalistic societies are said to belong to the former, setting up mechanisms to control deviants from the norm, while socialistic ones have mechanisms to prevent deviations from the start. In cultures that consider people to be untrustworthy, well-meaning controllers flourish.

There is a similar polarization in attitudes with respect to the consumer, except that it does not go along political lines. The consumer is seen as essentially wise or stupid. The former favors the term "consumer sovereignty," while the latter is paternalistic and, for the consumer's own "protection," limits the area of choice, which is the Japanese case. The foremost protector of the consumer from the predatory activities of the marketers in Japan is the Fair Trade Commission (FTC), against which I took issue earlier in this chapter.

As noted, moderately large premium offers are out, but, until recently, coupons did not exist either. Yes, those little slips that Americans, British, Australian, and many other consumers busily clip to present to their retailers. The FTC ruled not long ago that this form of promotion was not illegal within certain rules, but so far, only a limited number of magazines have accepted ads with coupons. The proviso here is that coupons must not be used as a vehicle to increase the circulation of the print medium. The rationale is that consumers should be buying the medium for its content, not because it offers coupons. This is strange, when considering the content of some popular magazines.

The Newspaper Association is currently debating whether to accept coupon advertising, the most important media for it in the U.S., with magazines accounting for only a fraction of it. By Western logic, this is also strange, because the one thing the print media offers that TV cannot is coupons; so it is a revenue-raising device for the media. Once again, the consumer is left out of the debate.

Coupons create a powerful device to accelerate the trial of new products, since a consumer who may hesitate to pay the full price for an unknown brand may be tempted through a discount coupon. The restriction placed by the FTC is that, similar to the magazine case, marketers should compete on product quality rather than by offering baits to consumers who may be tempted into buying something they do not need. Furthermore, even now the stance is that coupons should apply only to the first purchase and not be used as a tool to "force" consumers into repeat purchases by persuading them to accumulate coupons until the total reaches a certain redeemable value.

The FTC argument misses the point, in that couponing is an expense to the marketer that has to be recouped through subsequent purchases. If the product is not liked after trial, the consumer will not repurchase. Therefore, a marketer is competing on quality when he offers coupons. Anyway, the FTC is not noted for its logical consistency. For example, it allows discounting at the store level, but not through premiums, or, until recently, couponing, which is nothing more than discounting. Earlier, the FTC said that unlimited coupons could be handed to the consumer on the street but not in or just outside the store, since this links the action directly to sales. Yet it is perfectly all right for the storekeeper to offer discounts.

Many foreign marketers who are disdvantaged in accessing the trade have direct mass access to the consumer through couponing. Curbside distribution can hardly match the power of an ad in a mass circulation daily. Is it only coincidental that the trade prefers discounting, which it can control, to couponing? The benefit from the latter passes mostly to the consumer. Couponing also threatens market incumbents who would prefer not to be disturbed. But discouragement of this method of promotion deprives consumers of the opportunity of trying out a new product at the manufacturer's expense. Who is being protected?

Emerging Consumer Power

Changing the Japanese Market Infrastructure?

THERE IS MUCH TALK about the feudal nature of the Japanese market structure. Japan's rigid vertical networks, known as *keiretsu*, have given cause for such complaints. By definition, changes in the feudal structure can only be initiated from the top, and not from the grass roots. However, there is a growing realization that this system is too rigid to cope with the changing social environment—particularly, the pressures toward what is called "internationalization"; likewise, the emergence of the new consumer is at last creating a force from the bottom up, a force that can be formidable, as other advanced societies have found.

The food industry is especially vulnerable to the elements that are affecting the Japanese consumer market: the increased consumer preference toward value-added rather than cost-evaluated products; the individualization of tastes with a consequent fragmentation of markets; and the rapidly aging population, with increasing concerns toward health, etc. Manufacturers, faced with a mature market, are struggling to find new ways to grow by adapting to the new consumer. This has resulted in stirrings to link up with those in segments other than their own for access to know-how. In other words, horizontal rather than the traditional vertical relationships are developing.

It is said that some 3,500 to 4,000 new packaged food items enter the market annually; their survival rate is less than 10%. Moves will certainly be afoot for firms to combine their know-how to minimize the risk. Major manufacturers are seeking out relatively small manufacturers of daily food items to fill the gap in their product range. A case in point is a tie-up between Myojo Foods and Asahi Foods to establish a joint venture, Shanghai Foods, by the former buying the latter's production facilities in Kochi prefecture. Asahi Foods is a wholesaler that handles a full range of daily serving items, from frozen salted squid to fresh fish and vegetables. However, it is the first time that this company will be entering the manufacturing fray, through the Myojo tie-up. Myojo, a large manufacturing concern of dry packaged foods, has lacked the know-how to produce a wide range of frozen items.

Nor is the giant Ajinomoto company exempt from this trend. One of its subsidiaries has entered into joint development with Nihon Shokudo, a restaurant chain. The two intend to create an integrated system pooling market research, concept development, menu formulation, service, training, etc.

The fragmentation of consumer tastes is not only forcing manufacturers to re-evaluate their traditional forms of operation, but is also forcing them to radically alter product lines. Although corporate alignments may in fact have been accused of being feudalistic, within the system, individual manufacturers have demonstrated their flexibility in the past. Now that the Japanese consumers are moving less *en masse*, manufacturers must meet the real challenge to their marketing flexibility.

A number of major food manufacturers other than Ajinomoto—Itoh Meat Packers, Marudai Foods, Nippon Meat Packers, Nisshin Foods, Prima Ham, QP, etc.—are reported to have instituted strategies to strengthen their sales in the frozen foods area, which is necessitated by the trend away from dry items. Traditionally, this category has been left to small manufacturers; but stores, forced to cope with the fragmentation of consumer tastes, have decreased the shelf space devoted to dried packaged food in order to allow for extra displays of the many new frozen items. Such product fragmentation is threatening the survival of some food manufacturers.

Feudalistic structures require strength at the top. "When on to a good thing, stick to it," seemed to be the Japanese credo. But some industry leaders are being shaken by the new consumers, who are demonstrating that they couldn't care less whether a particular brand happened to be the leader for as long as they remember. Shiseido, the giant cosmetics firm, had its worst year ever in 1987. The giant Kirin Brewery seemed unperturbed towards all challenges until 1987. Complacent with a market share of around 60% for many years, it has been somewhat detached from the power of consumer pull. The hot summer of 1987 was a record-breaking year for beer sales. But the new record was also created by a proliferation of new brands from Kirin's three competitors and imports, stinging the market leader to react at last. All the activity enormously stimulated consumer interest in this category.

When the dust settled with the cooling autumn breezes, the top gainer was Asahi, which was shedding its image as a perennial loser. Headed by a new president acutely conscious of this fact, Asahi embarked upon a corporate identity program and came out with a super winner—Asahi Super Dry, a draft beer launched in March 1987. This phenomenon has been discussed separately as the decline of the megabrands.

Look out market incumbents! The new consumer will no longer follow you blindly.

Still Saving for a Rainy Day

A strange thing thing happned to me while I was listening to the noted commentator Kenichi Takemura deliver his opening statement in a television symposium in early 1988. Takemura came on strong, quoting a January 18, 1988, *Business Week* article that said that "this triumph over the high yen" is "Japan's second miracle, comparable to the nation's emergence from the ashes of war." This, of course, only proves the penchant among some American commentators to jump to quick conclusions. The Church takes a lot more time before it pronounces a miracle.

"Happiness is in spending" said Takemura, and his remark took me back to a school room in prewar Japan where thrift had been discussed as a virtue. "We save too much," said this popular commentator who has never been afraid to go against official pronouncements. But this time he was totally secure, since this agreement with the "unofficial" Maekawa Report—quoted more than any "official" report I have ever known—has been adopted as the party line. "The Americans have always had their dream; it is now time for us to have one," he emphasized. Just in case Japanese consumers did not get the point, his latest book was called "The Japanese Dream." With many books now focused on this new phenomenon called *shōhishakai* (consumer society), great curiosity is

being aroused on what would become of Japanese societal values if
people spent more and saved less.

Of course, in a war-footing economy, consumer spending is
discouraged. Those in the West had been exhorted to buy war
bonds, but in Japan, it started early in the schools. While still in
shorts, I was instilled with the ideas of Kinjirō Ninomiya. I have
forgotten most of the things taught in my ethics class—my
Australian mother went about undoing whatever was taught
there—but Ninomiya stuck, which suggests that the indoctrination
was pretty thorough.

Ninomiya (1787–1856) was an agrarian administrator—a
euphemism for a large landholder—who lived during the latter
period of the Tokugawa shogunate. Although his family had gone
bankrupt during his infancy, he studied hard and through skimping
and saving, he more than restored the family fortune. The only thing
that remains with me—and with most Japanese, too—is that he led
the way in preaching the virtue of thrift.

It crossed my childish mind at the time that I would never want to
meet this guy, since he would probably find a reason to confiscate my
pocket money. The West has billionaires who continue to make
money while never spending on private luxuries, but they are not
elevated as national idols. The label they earn is more likely to be
"miser."

In the early 1970s, I participated in a daytime TV panel sponsored
by the National Savings Associaton. Not surprisingly, the Association was funded by the banks. When I blurted out, after seeing the
commercial, "My God, are you still pushing Kinjirō Ninomiya?",
the sponsor was not amused.

Programmed teaching on the virtues of thrift suddenly
ceased—probably with the Maekawa Report. However, Ninomiya

re-emerged on a television program called "The Anatomy of Japan" broadcast nationally in late 1986. I was confronting a noted econometrician from a major Japanese brokerage house and raised the matter of saving rates. With an un-Japanese abruptness that surprised me and startled the director, he snapped, "There is nothing wrong with a high savings rate." Of course, he is right in the absolute sense. The Japanese are supposed to be relativists, but not on this issue. I dropped the matter because I knew that all I would get would be a lecture on the profligacy of the American consumer. But here was Ninomiya sitting in an NHK studio in the guise of a Japanese broker!

So, is Takemura advocating something that goes totally against the Japanese national character? Not entirely. Again, I remember a song that was quite popular in Japan in my school days. It concerned a guy called Shōsuke Ohara who was considered to be the epitome of slothfulness, a sort of Japanese Oblomov (a late Tsarist anti-hero who took to bed because he did not want to face the world). I found Oblomov in my Japanese encyclopedia but not Ohara; maybe the latter will be included in a later edition. Of course, Ohara came to no good end, but apparently had some fun riding to his doom. During those austere war years, probably many secretly yearned to be an Ohara rather than a Ninomiya. I understand that there was a song for Ninomiya too, sponsored by the Ministery of Education, but it certainly lacked popularity even at the time and has not endured like the one for Ohara.

Are the majority of Japanese consumers turning into Oharas? For various reasons, including macro-economic ones, not yet. But enough so that Ninomiya has started to disappear from the textbooks. There are always Ninomiyas and Oharas among us. I know which one I would choose to be with during my non-working hours. Quite simply, despite his glaring faults, Ohara would be more fun. More of Ohara and less of Ninomiya would make the Japanese consumer more fun to be with—and maybe we could say it represents a more positive part of "internationalizaton."

Pay Now, Consume Later is the Japanese Way

Foreign governments have been complaining about the Japanese bureaucracy's slowness in responding to their demands for the removal of controls. For example, the "Large Stores Act," introduced to protect small mom-and-pop stores (and thus perpetuate the inefficiency in distribution), has been under review and attack for some time. On the other hand, it seems that new controls are sometimes instituted with surprising ease, especially when compared to the resistance they usually meet in the United States. Faith in bureaucracy here is such that both industry and consumer cooperate with alacrity when the bureaucratic clarion sounds.

This time around it is MITI (Ministry of International Trade and Industry), which organized a "Gathering of Card Businesses" in December 1988. The meeting was dutifully attended by 70 odd organizations — including the Japan Chamber of Commerce, Japan Association of Department Stores, card producers, and representatives of distribution, printing, and banking. The speed in organizing the gathering is said to have surprised the Ministry of Finance, which is even more involved in the issue.

Big time "card business" in the United States is associated with credit cards. Here it refers to the opposite — "pre-paid cards." Facing stupendous growth, the Finance Ministry is rightly concerned that a new form of currency has emerged and apparently feels that controls should be imposed before things get out of hand. According to the Japanese press, MITI too is worried, but on another score: that there may be eventual bankruptcies, hurting some consumers in the wake. This prompted MITI's sponsoring of the industry meeting, without reference to Finance, so that a degree of self-discipline could be exercised. MITI, unlike Finance, wants to respect the vitality of the private business sector, viewing the growth of pre-paid card as an inevitable consequence of business activities.

The genesis of the current controversy is in the issuance of pre-paid telephone cards. MITI estimates that well over five hundred million pre-paid telephone cards have been issued since 1982, 228 million of them in 1987 alone, up 50% from 1986, i.e., accelerating rapidly in the latest years.

The cultural twist is that, in the West, you make a phone call on credit; in Japan you pay up first and leave most of the consuming to the future. For the issuer of the card, it is indeed a license to print money, in the same league as travelers' checks. But cards are easier to use because verification is not required. The common telephone card costs ¥1,000, so to use it up, you have to make 100 local calls from the roughly one in every three public phone booths that are currently equipped to handle the card. With commendable business acumen, NTT, the newly privatized telephone company, aims to raise this ratio to 50% by March 1989.

The Japanese, showing a genius for building on a good idea, latched on to the fact that cards could be made with appealing designs, or better still, a company's identification. After all, Japan is a gift culture, *par excellence*. Telephone cards make a better publicity medium than even pocket diaries or calenders. You can personally use only a few of the latter, so the competition for attention among them is severe. However, an unused telephone card is not thrown out and stays in the wallet as a frequent reminder of the given. I, together with most Japanese businessmen, have a pocket full of them and now have little use for ten-yen coins, except when traveling by taxi, because now there are pre-paid railway cards, too. The railways, public as well as private, are very good at issuing commemorative cards. A long distance rail trip is almost certain to have a guard coming around peddling one of them.

Commemorative telephone cards also abound at weddings and children's birthday or graduation parties — with portrait photographs, of course, for remembrance of the giver. Pre-paid cards, like postage stamps, have become collectors' items and grace albums, after or even before use. Their strong integration into the gift market can be judged by the sharp drop in sales reported in recent periods, along with festive food such as prawns and bream, because of the cancellation of receptions due to the late Emperor's illness at the time.

Pre-paid cards now cover the whole gamut, from pachinko parlors to hamburgers. And now, the jumbo pre-paid card has arrived. Fukuzakaya supermarket in Osaka is issuing one with a face value of ¥100,000, discounted to ¥91,000 (although one has the choice of smaller denominations). Unlike a store credit card which may occasionally be defaulted, it is a safe bet with the customer's money in the pocket.

The concept has now been extended to an entire shopping block. The Kasumigaseki Building — once the tallest office building in Tokyo in an area where government departments concentrate — has introduced a *biru kado* (building card). It can be used in any of the 37 stores, 4 vending machines and the parking ticket dispenser in the building. No longer a king among Tokyo skyscrapers, the building has sharply lost sightseers and it is hoped that the card will help revive business.

Where else but Japan would paying first and consuming later be so attractive? I don't see the gap in the savings rate between the United States and Japan narrowing — left to natural inclinations, that is.

PART FIVE

THE SEE-SAW OF CHANGE

FORCES AGAINST THE SHINJINRUI

The Educational Battle Ground

I HAVE LONG ARGUED that to truly understand the Japanese employer, worker, and consumer, it is necessary to understand Japan's education system. However, its fundamental differences with that of the West are not understood by most Japanese, let alone foreigners. Few will disagree that education was one of the major contributors to Japan's industrial success, by having the most educated work force in the world. Japanese children spend more time away from their homes than most Western children and more time with an intensely target-oriented group of peers, a large proportion working toward the goal of entering a college. The renowned "quality circles" work better here than in the West, because of strong target and group orientations developed during school days.

Much of the talk about an emerging "new breed" of consumers is based on observations of behavior patterns of the young, who are enjoying a brief period of freedom. The fact that they constitute the first generation to be without the hangups caused by insecurity is important. However, the almost Pavlovian reflexes created through the intensive periods up to high school will remain, and as the education system stands, neither economic wealth nor those package tours abroad are going to turn the Japanese consumers into replicas of Americans.

The fall sees the annual open hunt for students by corporations. For a student, it is the time when those long years of arduous work, spanning from primary to high school—with a breather during college—bear or do not bear fruit. This is when, as a president of a small non-Japanese company, I used to feel sadly left out. For a long time, we were not in the bidding for fresh graduates. Our management was delighted this year, to have applicants straight from the colleges; it has only taken us twenty years to be accepted as part of the community!

The Japanese say they live in a *gakureki shakai*, meaning a society based on scholastic careers. No wonder they take a keen interest in what is going on in education. When the John Naisbitt-style of content analysis is applied to the Japanese news media, education looms as a major category often occupying the front page lead in the major dailies. For example, education-related matters were very much in the news in the fall of 1986. A decidedly right-leaning Mr. Fujio, Minister of Education, was fired for his outrageous remarks in a monthly magazine that there was collusion, albeit minor, on the Korean side in its past annexation by Japan. The decidedly left-leaning Teachers' Federation split into an acrimonious dispute, as leftists are prone the world over. Both were transitory events and now are not even old news. However, long term shifts of great significance are occurring in the education field which will affect future societal values and, hence, corporate and consumer attitudes.

The news that the rate of entry into universities had dropped by a whopping 2.9 points to 34.7 percent in one year was seen as the inability of the universities to absorb the increased numbers due to carry over births from the year following *hinoe-uma*—an astrologically unlucky year for girls. However, there has been a long-term decline in the rate from a peak of 38.6 percent in 1976, with one short recovery in between. Interestingly, the slack has been taken up by entry into technical schools rather than universities. It could be that some at least are giving up on the intensive pressure for passing the entrance exams to colleges that provide a general education. Could this be a gradual shift toward specialization from the generalist bent? Specialists tend to be more individualistic and occupation, rather than corporation, oriented.

Another news item of interest was that the National PTA met during mid-August of 1986 to discuss the *gakureki shakai* and the effect it has on both children and families. There was an explosion of mistrust from the parents toward the once sacrosanct teaching profession, the most important outcry concerning the issue of regimentation and authoritarian tyranny. Individual comments, describing treatments meted out to their children, read like something out of Charles Dickens. Corporal punishment in schools remains a hot issue in 1988, with many actually arguing for its retention.

Activist parents who turn out at such meetings are hardly typical. There are strong revisionist moves, away from what is perceived as a MacArthur–enforced system and toward further regimentation, to eliminate violence in the schools. Presumably, Mr. Fujio would have continued as Minister of Education for a while if he had not been fired because of his indiscreet remarks about Korea. But there were other things he said that are worth quoting and that could be suspected of being mainstream thinking. "Postwar education was instituted to destroy Japan," he said, astonishingly, considering

Japan's achievements. "What about prewar education, which led to the war?" asks "Vox Populi," a liberal *Asahi* columnist. The same Mr. Fujio is all in favor of reinstituting the Imperial prescript on education that will foster national pride. There is clearly a tug of war going on. But narrow nationalism will not win. Japan has gone too far toward becoming an international society to let it happen.

Cultural Insularity—Unofficial Part of Japanese School Curriculum?

Approximately one year after penning the above, I˙ was quickly reminded of the tug of war going on between the new generation and the conservative forces in education. I went through the pre-1945 Japanese school system, so there was a feeling of déjà vu when I came across a passage in a serialized novel in the *Asahi*. The novel, entitled *Yellow Hair,* was by the young author Hikari Agata and ran in the paper in 1987. It featured a senior high-school girl call-ed Natsumi who would be labeled by many now as *shinjinrui* (new breed).

The girl is detached and cynical, far more than any student in my day, but the teacher, on the other hand, was clearly recognizable from World War II days. Here is just a short extract to give you a taste of the situation:

(The students are lined up for dress inspection.) "All right," said the teacher, who then moved on. Haruo Sugiura, who was next, had a hairstyle that was somewhat different. His father's income was unstable and there were four kids in the family, so his mother trimmed his hair with scissors. The teacher passed by him without saying "All right." He shoved his right hand into the hair of the next boy and smoothed down the part that was sticking up, with his left. "Kanda. Are you too busy with *juku* (private cram school) to go to the barber's?" "I will go today, sir," said Takashi Kanda, who topped the class in grades, in a deep voice.

The kid with the wrong hairdo is asked formally, when the teacher goes to the platform, if he had submitted an "application for different attire." It appears that such a rule is most often applied when the uniform is sent out to the cleaners and one is forced to deviate in appearance from the norm. To prevent "misunderstandings," it is advisable for girls with curly hair to notify the school at the time of their entry of this condition, so that they will not be accused of having their hair permed—a breach of school rules. Heaven help the girl who has hair that is not naturally black, as bleaching or dyeing would be a serious violation. Presumably, she would not be challenged if her hair was dyed unnoticeably black!

Here is a startling reminder of the Japanese dislike of differences in their midst. The renowned Japanese group conformity continues to be fostered solidly during school years, and the *shinjinrui* are even now subjected to this pressure. It would seem that they are fighting back only passively, which is not surprising, as the penalties for overt resistance are severe. When we talk about change wrought by the new generation of Japanese, we tend to play down the counterforces lined up against them.

Clearly, one needs to understand the Japanese education system to comprehend current Japanese attitudes. But for predicting changes in cultural values, it is crucial to know what is going on. In analyzing carefully the contents of print media to see what is driving Japan toward basic changes, it becomes clear that education is emerging as a critical trend factor.

The debate is furious and there are reformers in both camps: those who would like to emphasize or reinforce traditional values and those who would like to "modernize" the system and encourage a less insular or group-oriented attitude.

There is a tug of war going on for the hearts and minds of the *shinjinrui*, which continues into the work place, after graduation. Observing them on the streets of Tokyo's trendy suburb of Harajuku—which catches them at their freest moments in life—somehow exaggerates the differences from their predecessors and their immediate impact on society.

As long as teachers and schools of the kind described above are in the majority, so-called modernists are engaged in an uphill struggle. And like a Pavlovian response, from the first day in a corporation, it's back to school, and the Harajuku—a trendy suburb—days are but a memory. But can this attitude survive in the information age? No—and that's what the fuss is all about.

Pressures and Reactions:
"Internationalization"—But How Far?

Reality and Expectations

UNCONNECTED RELEASES by the Japanese government departments revealed a gap between the perceptions of officials and the man on the street. The Economic Planning Agency's report on "Technological Innovations and Employment" in May 1986 forecasted dramatic structural changes in the years to come, but the Japanese have proven themselves very adept at that. According to the report, numbers employed in the tertiary industry will increase from about 31 million in 1980 to over 41 million in the year 2000, accounting for two in three employed versus slightly over half now. This sector will be divided roughly equally between distribution and information-related activities—the latter are those who do not physically handle goods, neither in their making nor in transporting them to the user. Even in the declining manufacturing sector, there will be a shift into research, development, and marketing.

The Agency is optimistic that the decline in primary and secondary industry workers and the increase in the work force—about 8 million—will be compensated for by the growing tertiary sector. Japan has gone through such rapid changes in the past—in thirty years from agrarian employment to light industry to heavy industry, with always a large underpinning in the distribution sector. First, the industrialization of the consumer led to a heavy demand on consumer durables, then the urbanization of the consumer led to diversification of demand and sensitivity toward non-utilitarian values. In the market place, the shift has been from "distribution push" to "consumer pull." In the former, the emphasis was on placing products on the shelves, whereas in the latter, it is in creating and communicating appeals to the consumer. If the balance of power shifts more to the consumer from the trade, this will help foreign manufacturers. However, just *when* consumer sovereignty will reign remains to be seen. The Agency, being a body of macro-economic analysts, coolly points out that the consequence of such a shift is the creation of greater opportunity to select one's occupation and that this may have an impact on the lifetime employment system. An increase in specialists and a reduction in generalists is implied—the very antithesis of current Japanes practice, but I have earlier noted a shift from general college education toward specialized technical education. The character of the work will be transformed, as, *ipso facto*, that of the consumer. Occupational environment affects attitudes; accountants and lawyers seem to develop certain idiosyncrasies. So when there is a change in work environment at a national level, we need to know its ramifications on the market.

One's attitude toward work itself, however, is not determined by one's occupation. Two of the greatest workaholics I ever met in a Western corporation were polar opposites in terms of what they did: one was an engineer working alone on design projects, and the other, an entrepreneur dedicated to moving people around. A shift in the industrial structure will not automatically change the Japanese from workaholics to leisure seekers. This brings me to the second piece from the government, "A Survey of Attitudes Toward Leisure and Travel," conducted by the Prime Minister's department during January 1986, a follow-up of surveys conducted in 1979 and 1982.

Despite the notorious lack of it, when asked whether they would like to have more leisure time, half of the males in their forties and fiftis said that they were satisfied with the current state. A reduction in working hours is now seen as a means of alleviating trade friction. It seems, however, that you can lead middle-aged Japanese workers to leisure, but you can't make them take it. More than 40% of this generation considered that "work is important and leisure time was for rest and change of mood for that end." Officially, taking off every Saturday and Sunday is on the increase, but this was not reflected in the surveys up to 1982, with less than 8% doing so.

Perhaps we can take heart in the fact that the balance is tipped toward leisure among the young respondents. The world is full of people who think that youthful attitudes herald a change in society, but they forget their own past. I, too, loved my days off when I was young, but these days I am said to be a typical Japanese workaholic. Who would have predicted the Yuppies at the time of the Flower Children? (With Black Monday, I now believe the Yuppies are out and Tweenies are in.) With its group pressures and its hierarchical structure, it is premature to say that this difference in generational attitudes alone suggests a breakdown in the Japanese work ethic. The apathy of the average worker toward gaining increased leisure time in return for his productivity is certainly one of the outstanding differences between Japan and the West.

However, it is hard to see how the kind of structural change the Economic Planning Agency foresees can be brought about without a modificatión of the work ethics. Quality circles with robots? A change in the way work is regarded would be as revolutionary as anything this country has seen in recent years. It means a fundamental change in the consumer and a transformation of the marketplace. If imposed through external pressure rather than evolving organically, there may be some turbulence. Japanese society traditionally strives to avoid major distrubances in its own way of life, so the tug of war will be interesting for the observer, but not necessarily for those involved.

In the Eye of a Storm of Change

Even as recently as 1986, the turbulence occurring within Japan was still a matter largely discussed by the Japanese themselves. Now, change is on everyone's mind, and it was especially so in Dublin in April 1987, when, at the instigation of Edward De Bono, who coined the phrase "lateral thinking," I joined others invited to discuss the subject.

Interestingly, business chiefs and consultants welcomed change and were optimistic about the future. The former are risk-takers and must be optimistic, while the latter serve the risk-takers. The pessimists involved included economists and bureaucrats.

Maxwell Newton, a Murdoch columnist (*New York Post, London Times,* etc.) painted a vivid picture of the world in the hands of money men intent only on the short term and teetering on the brink as a result. The Japanese, he emphasized, had joined the destabilizing money game, with companies hitherto geared to export, now speculating on the stock market. He even seemed to predict the stock market crash in October 1987. William Nickerson Walker (a former ambassador, head of the U.S. delegation to the Multinational Trade Negotiations and chief U.S. negotiator at the Tokyo Rounds) described the U.S. and Japan as inexorably heading toward a trade impasse.

Japan was much on the minds of both men, Newton ascribing to the prevalent view of a mercantilist state that has delivered the current crisis because of its self-serving economic policies. I naturally found myself pricking up my ears everytime someone said "Japan,"—and that was quite often.

It has not always been like this. It does not seem so long ago that I attended an international conference in Zurich where one speaker did not even include Japan on a map used to discuss international marketing!

This time, in Dublin, there was hardly a speaker who did not touch on Japan. When I finally got up to speak, I was afraid that the subject had been overaired. I had left Japan on a Saturday with the yen at 140 to the dollar; after the weekend it raced to 137; then back to 139 on Tuesday. But, of course, this was not the sort of change with which the conference was concerned.

With the human fascination for numbers, one speaker kept referring to the year 2000, as if these round numbers portend any particular significance. He declared that by that year, Japan would no longer be No. 1, but about No. 16 in ranking. He also emphasized Japan's ethnic homogeneity, and stated that this is the great unknown in the current challenge for Japan to internationalize.

There is ample evidence that Japan will resist cultural pollution from outside and, needless to say, its ethnic purity will be protected with vehemence. While De Bono lauded Japan for flexibility, on this matter the nation remains staunchly inflexible, and, of course, this is a choice the Japanese are entitled to make—although with the understanding that they will have to sacrifice on other matters. Australia made a choice in the other direction and has survived well as a society.

In fact, a distinguished Frenchman attending the Dublin conference questioned me in no uncertain terms regarding the spate of anti-Semitic books in Japan at the time that suggest "To understand the world, you have to understand the Jews." Although I had recently written on this phenomenon, I struggled with a short response.

It amounts to a cultural backlash stemming from "threats" imposed from outside. Words such as "adversarial" and "retaliatory" sound extremely bad in Japanese, and the community at large feels put upon. And it is particularly tough coming from Japan's great and admired friend, the Americans.

The publications in question have latched onto American Jewry as an abstraction and as a convenient label that suggests it is only a conspiratorial portion of the United States that has turned against the Japanese. As such, it must not be confused with the abominable racism that manifested itself in Hitler's Germany. Unfortunately, my questioner seemed unconvinced.

On the whole, conferees were optimistic on "change." Steven Falken, president of Dealing With Change, Inc. (could it be anything but American?) was the most optimistic, contending that change was a matter of perception and could always be turned to the good. While those in some East European countries may disagree, his quotation of management guru Peter Drucker seemed an appropriate summation of enterpreneurial attitudes: "The first step in a global strategy is to decide what to abandon." To that I would add another Druckerism: "We spend too much time solving problems when we should be chasing opportunities."

Cultural Homogeneity and the Fear of Contamination

The two buzz words in the Japanese media in 1986–87 were *shinjinrui* ("the new breed") and *kokusaika* ("internationalization"). The first suggested an organic change, while the second was related to foreign pressure through the trade imbalance, that is, an inorganic change. The big question emerging now is whether "internationalization" can be ultimately realized without disturbing the so-called Japanese cultural homogeneity.

Change is a historical inevitability, but most societies prefer it to be gradual. If Japan's experiences of the recent past are taken as an example, a sharp change is a stimulant that propels society. On the other hand, the Iran example would seem to prove otherwise. The Japanese trick was to take in Western technology without affecting societal values. The key to this riddle, as is well recognized, is the lack of religion, or the absence of absolute precepts, and a disposition to evaluate phenomena in relative and pragmatic terms. If circumstances change, Japan changes directions. Neither Khomeini's Iran nor Marxist USSR can do that because they have absolutes to which they have to adhere. But even the Japanese will react if their social values are challenged too suddenly.

Some Westerners who thought the Shah was marvelous failed to see that he was pushing it too quickly and that there would be a massive reaction. The world is the worse for it. The unfortunate thing for the Japanese is that the West sees it on the defensive, and wants to keep pressing. In the current pressure for "internationalization," the biggest problem is that nobody has really defined the term. There is no such thing as absolute "internationalization." Do we mean that all societies are going to be like all others? If it means peace on earth, that is a worthy goal.

However, if it means that some dominant economic or military power dictates that everyone else should be like itself, then, far from peace, there is going to be trouble. Despite intellectual commentators who predict that the ill-defined "internationalization" is a good goal to work toward, apprehension is developing in Japan, and it is taking two forms. One blames the threat on a sinister conspiracy that raises the dark specter of the Weimer and Hitler, on which I was questioned at the international conference. The other aspect concerns cultural contamination: that "internationalization" will disturb Japan's cultural "purity." This manifestests itself in the proposition that foreign products, let alone foreigners, are dangerous. The Japanese Consumer Union's pamphlet on unsafe foreign food products is a good example.

Professor Emeritus Aida of Kyoto University writes in the magazine *Voice* that the USA symbolizes AIDS, and implies that Americanization, which he seems to equate with "internationalization," will erode the moral fiber of Japanese society. What is preached here is nationalism, the very antithesis of the "expected." These are the inevitable reactions of old men afraid of change. Still, Japanese society is being challenged full force on values that it believes to be unique and the best for humanity. Indeed, the West could do with many of these values. But equally, Japan cannot have things all its way. Absolutist stands on either side will do no good. The cliche stands—these are troubled times when cool heads should prevail.

Assuming World Leadership

Prime Minister Yasuhiro Nakasone's remark that the average American intellectual standard is lower than that of the average

Japanese standard because of the blacks and Hispanics in the U.S. surprised few in Japan. Made at a speech to an inner circle of followers with Japanese journalists present, it went virtually unreported in Japan until a foreign journalist got hold of it and there was a subsequent uproar in the U.S. The world reaction became news here in turn.

Many Japanese, not least Mr. Nakasone, were shocked by the world's response. Mr. Nakasone had positioned himself for leading Japan into the international community, so he was greatly disturbed that his remarks were "misinterpreted." In his view, he was expressing compassion for a great friend and was glad that his country did not have America's problems.

Mr. Nakasone has often said that the source of Japan's strength lies in its "racial homogeneity" (a euphemism for "racial purity"), a view that is widely shared. His mistake this time was that instead of talking about racial purity as a general principle, he compared Japan with the U.S. and named blacks and Hispanics.

I must confess that had I been there when Mr. Nakasone made his comment, I too, would have let it pass. All foreigners living in Japan become resigned to the fact that they will always be *gaijin* (literally, "outsiders) welcome as temporary visitors but never admitted to the village community. Despite the purported "internationalism" of many Japanese, it rarely extends beyond such superficialities as wearing French clothes, enjoying Italian opera, or eating American fast food. The average Japanese will instinctively avoid close contact with foreigners, an attitude that is not so much racism as a fear of the unknown.

In my own case, having been born and educated in Japan and speaking accentless Japanese doesn't make me any less of an outsider. In June, for instance, I read a paper at an international marketing conference in Tokyo. The paper was in English, the official language of the conference, and was simultaneously translated into Japanese. As papers of this kinds are prone to, it had some jargon for which my interpreter sought clarification; she expected it to be in English. I decided that it was more logical to clarify the items in Japanese. But when I had finished, she looked at me in a strange way and exclaimed, "Oh, you give me the creeps!" In other words, no "foreigner" should speak exactly like a Japanese.

It is as hard for a Japanese to understand that somebody would want to be one of them—a sheer contradiction in terms to them—as it is for an American to imagine that every immigrant does not want eventually to become an American. I was standing on a New York street corner during the 1968 Nixon-Humphrey presidential race when I was approached by a campaign worker. "Vote for Nixon," she said, thrusting a leaflet in my hand. I returned it to her murmuring. "Sorry, I can't." She looked at me alarmed. "Why's that?" "Because I'm not American." As she moved away I heard her say, "Oh, well, better luck next time." As I explain this story to my Japanese audience, Americans think everybody is going to be like them one day. Whereas in Japan, foreigners are supposed to go back to where they came from sooner or later.

There is one substantial group of "foreigners" made up of those who cannot go back to where they came from. It comprises some 700,000 Koreans, many of whom were forcibly brought here as laborers during Japan's 1910–45 occupation of their country. Their children and grandchildren, even though they were born here and have never known another home, cannot automatically become Japanese, since citizenship is based on bloodline. While it's possible for them to become naturalized citizens, not all do, presumably because they know that they'll never be accepted as "true" Japanese, despite the fact that in appearance and speech they seem so. Employers and potential spouses routinely hire investigators to look into an applicant's background and if they find out that someone is of Korean ancestry, that is almost always a black mark against him.

Koreans are not the only local residents who face discrimination. Others include Indo-Chinese refugees, of whom Japan has accepted less than 5,000; a small Chinese community; a group of indigenous people called the Ainu, who live on the northern island of Hokkaido; and the *burakumin,* an underclass of scorned ancestry rather like India's untouchables. Even Japanese children who live abroad for a few years and attend local schools there have trouble reentering Japanese society because they have been "contaminated."

Possibly the first foreigner to suffer such discrimination was Lafcadio Hearn, an Irish-Greek-American writer who lived in Japan at the turn of the century. (Hearn's unhappy fascination with Japan is what some longtime foreign residents here call "Hearnia.")

At first, Hearn was totally enamored of Japanese culture, and his early writings were masterpieces of evocation. He was rejecting his own culture, and everything he saw in Japan seemed a fulfillment of his dreams. He married a Japanese woman, and did an unusual thing—became a naturalized Japanese and changed his name to Yakumo Koizumi. Although Hearn had little formal education, he could write, and he was recommended to a professorship at the prestigious Tokyo Imperial University by the renowned Orientalist, Basil Hall Chamberlain, who was returning to England. But Hearn's mistake may have been becoming Japanese, or so he thought.

His salary was promptly reduced because he was no longer a foreigner. But the final blow came a few years later, when the Ministry of Education decided that all professors must be Japanese and Hearn was fired. He protested that he had taken out Japanese citizenship. But the administrators shrugged and said, "How can you be Japanese? Your eyes are blue." He died a few years later, a very bitter man. End of a great Japanese romance.

Japan does not have a monopoly on racism, of course, as Prince Philip's 1986 remark to British students in China about "slitty eyes" reminds us. This comment struck a particularly bitter note, since many Asians recall the indignities and slights they have suffered from Westerners in recent history. Many Japanese, for instance, remember Gen. Douglas MacArthur's comparison of the average Japanese to a 12-year-old.

In the end, Mr. Nakasone may have done the Japanese a service by speaking as bluntly as he did. If anything, the world response should signal to them that their values are at odds with those of the rest of the world, however sophisticated Japan may be in terms of economics, politics, or trade. The shocked reactions may be a reminder to the Japanese that they shouldn't make the same mistake they made in the 1930s and 1940s, when racism led to Japan's deplorable behavior toward other Asians. Japan can become a leader of the world community only if it can shed this nonsense about the inherent superiority of the Japanese people. Their remarkable economic achievements are due to cultural values that produced an efficient manufacturing system and are not due to racial excellence.

Another Slip of the Tongue

Keizō Saji, president of the giant alcoholic beverage marketer Suntory, made a remark in early 1988 that recalls former Prime Minister Yasuhiro Nakasone's slip regarding minority groups in the U.S. that caused the backlash there. The remarks causing the furor in the entire northeastern Tōhoku region of Japan, like those of Nakasone, were made in a gathering of colleagues among which the speaker was in his element and extremely comfortable. Both speakers were probably attempting to provide an upbeat note to raise the spirits of the audience. And both remarks were off-the-cuff and unscripted, so could be suspected of revealing the speakers' true feelings.

Saji also happens to be the president of the Osaka Chamber of Commerce, the group to which he was speaking, and as a business leader in the western region, has been fighting the accelerating concentration of power into Tokyo. There is much talk now of shifting the capital from Tokyo elsewhere to counterbalance the trend, and some are carrying the torch for Sendai in the northeastern region. In a throwaway line, Saji said that it was nonsense to consider Sendai a rival. "After all," he stated, "it's Kumaso territory." The remark was caught by the TV cameras, and I happened to see the clip on my screen, but there was no comment at the time by the newscaster. As may have occurred with the Nakasone remark, if kept within the circle, it may not have been picked up as exceptional. But it turned out that it was broadcast nationally. While there were some titters in the Osaka audience Saji addressed, those in Tōhoku were outraged.

Actually, Saji didn't even get his anthropological facts straight. The Kumaso were an ancient tribe that originally lived in Kyushu, in southern Japan, not in Tōhoku. It is said that they resisted the power of the Yamato dynasty and were conquered in the third century, but there is no firm documentation and historians are now inclined to consider their existence a myth. While dictionaries carefully avoid any reference to prejudice, to be referred to as a Kumaso is to be labeled as uncouth, uneducated, and not socially acceptable. Nakasone talked about the blessing of a pure society with no internal conflict, but the Kumaso remark is no less racist than the slurs made against other groups in other cultures that are not so "blessed."

Saji clearly confused the Kumaso with another racial group, the Ezo, who are said to have established the agrarian culture in the Tōhoku region to which he referred. Many scholars believe they were the ancestors of the almost extinct Ainu, now living in a few parts of Hokkaido. Domestically, it was the Ainu who objected to Nakasone's remarks concerning a racially harmonious society.

Hispanics and blacks in the U.S. talked about boycotting Japanese products after the Nakasone incident, but exports were not affected. With many apologies and humbling on the part of Suntory, this affair will ultimately blow away for the company. What will not go away is the growing realization that put-downs by one group against another are neither funny nor acceptable, and that there is no longer any haven in the world for leaders who display condescension.

This is a new phenomenon. The weak within a culture and countries without strength have traditionally had to put up with slights from the dominant. But now changes are being triggered by the information society and, fundamentally, by the instant global transmission of information. Brought into our homes on TV, we can no longer view sanctimoniously the Jewish-Palestinian conflict as merely one involving two racial or religious groups. We see it for what it is—a real human tragedy. The world will no longer tolerate those who continue to make racist or sexist remarks in private. The circle is closing in.

"Race," "Sex," and "Internationalization"

One by one, taboo subjects are disappearing, but I suspect that some still remain. The traditional view is that the Japanese are not accustomed to open debate. But an unexpected consequence of "internationalization" is bringing to the forefront two aspects at the core of any modern society: the roles of race and sex. As a subject, the former has been virtually taboo, but both have been forced into the open by the verbal slips made by the eminent. I recently spoke to the staff of a manufacturing firm in provincial Japan that may have to move some of its production out of Japan. The company's concern was the consequent need to work with people of different cultural values. I pointed out that there are two rather unsavory words in the English language: "racist" and "sexist." Within a host culture, a proper understanding of their connotation is essential, as the terms are frequently the subject of open dispute.

To illustrate, I noted that among those gathered—from junior management up and numbering more than a hundred—there were neither any non-Japanese nor women. A truly multinational company would employ at least a sprinkling of both, a situation that would require a new mind-set in personnel management.

Lately I've been occupied with the fact that the issues of "race" and "sex" have merged to create controversy in the most unexpected quarters—the Japanese farm community. In many countries, the furious and open · debate here—Japanese farmers marrying Filipino and Thai women—is a non-event. In media circles, the phenomenon is described as a "bride famine" on the farms, created by the preference of the modern Japanese female for urban living. An unfortunate statement was made in public that love is secondary to the need for children and that "it does not matter where the bride comes from." In the West, the remark would be construed as both sexist and racist.

Marriages of convenience were the norm in feudalistic societies, but clearly Japan has abandoned the practice as indicated by the protest from women concerning the above-mentioned practice on several counts. First, there has been a commercialization in the process of arranging interracial marriages, with transactions by some shady operators, using women like commodities. Second, some women are being brought to Japan on the false pretense of a higher standard of living; the reality, of course, is glorified domestic labor. Finally, few women are properly prepared for the difficulties they will encounter in language and customs.

These points hardly address the core issues. Theoretically, they can be dealt with through appropriate controls to prevent the involvement of wrongdoers and through a proper period of orientation for the brides. After all, some may prefer work on Japanese farms to what they leave behind. Language, and, up to a point, customs can be learned. On these points alone it is understandable for the farmers involved to protest that it's no one else's business. Marriage is indeed a personal matter, so who should criticize?

But there is more to it than that. These personal dramas symbolize a society in transition. Farmers see themselves as victims of modernization, which has encroached on their dignity. They claim that the absence of a coherent farm policy has caused a deterioration of farm life, making it unattractive to the modern woman.

Modernization is also viewed as eroding important traditional values concerning family and motherhood. Questioned are concepts such as *ie* (home and family) and *yome* (bride) which are based on feudal values that placed women in a subservient position to the male head of the house, and where the primary role of the female was to bear and rear children for the purpose of continuing the line. Women can say that it is a matter of personal choice whether such values are embraced or not. The new Southeast Asian brides, too, are entitled to that choice.

So that is the "sex" side of the matter, which is being clearly addressed by the modern woman through open debate. However, by labeling these marriages *kokusai kekkon* (international marriages), an additional dimension is introduced. Looking through editorials, commentaries, and letters to the press, I have been struck by the almost total absence of a significant point: the ultimate effect of such marriages on the perception of Japan as a "homogeneous" (euphemism for "pure") society. After all, former Prime Minister Yasuhiro Nakasone did say that this was the source of Japan's strength.

On the same point, the difficulty of overseas-educated Japanese children adapting to the rules of Japanese society has been the subject of a highly rated television drama. Many schools specifically forbid children from looking different, particularly in dress and hairstyle. Born and bred in Japan, the offsprings of international marriages should have no problem adhering to the rules of society. But they will have trouble "looking the same."

Problems encountered after World War II by children of mixed blood are well known, but, undoubtedly, the trauma of defeat made things worse. Before the war, there were so few that they were mostly lumped in together with the foreigners and simply treated as curiosities.

I hasten to add that Japan is not the only society that shuns the "strange." After all, there is the Hans Christian Andersen tale about the ugly duckling. And yet, has this aspect not been raised in the current context because it is taboo—like the "non-existent" racial and other minorities in Japan—or has Japan entered a completely new phase in which "internationalization" of this kind will be taken in its stride?

As the children of international marriages on the farms grow up, and if they are noticeable in numbers, we will know the answer. It would be impressive if true internationalization emerges unself-consciously from the Japanese heartland. The consequences will be important for Japanese society and I fervently hope that the process will not be painful for those involved. If there is any chance of future ostracism of these children, the matter should be debated openly now.

However, judging from a television drama I watched subsequently, such a debate may be a while in coming. It was called "Goodbye Shaylen," aired during the peak viewing period over NHK, the national network. Shizuka was a housewife leading what could be described as an average, uneventful life. She had a past as a repatriate from Manchuria where presumably her parents had gone as migrants from a conquering power. She was separated from her parents and her brother during the ensuing chaos with the Imperial army in retreat and returned to Japan accompanied by a Japanese woman. However, the drama starts when a woman emerges from the past, operating a small bar in the neighborhood, who was on the same repatriation ship as Shizuka and remembered her as a small girl without a word of Japanese to her vocabulary. For some reason, this woman now pesters Shizuka, hinting that there was something unknown in her past. The drama reaches a high point when it is revealed that Shizuka is really Shaylen and Chinese.

Many Japanese are still traumatized when seeing, on TV, the annually organized visits from China of those of Japanese blood, now well into their forties, who were left behind at the time of the Japanese withdrawal. Of course, in speech, manner and dress, they are completely Chinese, which creates strong emotions in the Japanese viewer; understandably so for Shizuka, the central character in the drama, who could easily see herself as one of them. However, the bombshell in the drama is that Shizuka finds that she is in fact

Chinese by birth. Despite the fact that she is completely Japanese in life style, manner and values, the shock of the revelation almost deranges her and she wanders away from home and family, finding salvation among a group of what the Japanese call Chinese orphans — those who are Japanese by blood but not Japanese because of their speech and manners.

Since it concerned the Chinese and not the Europeans, the issue would, on the surface, seem not that of racial but cultural identity, but the Japanese make no such distinction in their perception of homogeneity. With the exception of Hitler's Germany, would any European be traumatized in adulthood to that extent when finding that his or her ancestry was not what had been originally expected? Shizuka or Shaylen's poignant cries on the TV screen were — "I can't be Chinese and I can't be Japanese, so what am I?" An American would be rightly puzzled and ask, "why can't you be Japanese?" The daughter in the drama, when discovering her own predicament as related to her mother, says she will apply to an American college. She dryly states: "Smarter to become an American than being half Japanese and half Chinese." This highly-rated drama was broadcasted in 1988.

The "Middle-Class" Society—For How Long?

Questionable Claims

ONE STATISTIC THAT IS quoted often in the annual survey on various attitudes toward livelihood conducted by the Prime Minister's office is that the great majority of Japanese think of themselves as belonging to the middle class. It is cited as yet another affirmation of the cultural homogeneity of Japanese society.

As a researcher, I have always been skeptical of the validity of this data. After all, in a society that goes by the saying, "The nail that sticks out gets hammered down," such an attitude would seem to be expected. In fact, most market researchers have discovered quite early that Japanese answers on any given question tend to cluster more toward the middle compared with international norms. I therefore have not been able to go along with Japanese commentators who proudly assert that to have more than 90% of the population in the middle class is an "amazing" political phenomenon.

Nevertheless, I took note of the great fuss being made of the fact that the number of those answering that they considered themselves "lower middle" has been gradually increasing, and now exceeds 30% in '87, according to the regular survey conducted by the Prime Minister's Office. The majority of slightly over 50% still consider themselves as "middle-middle." Since about 7% consider themselves as "upper middle," this still means that 90% classify themselves as "middle class." As I said before, I don't think this last figure is particularly amazing, considering the wordings of the question but importantly, those who considered themselves "middle-middle" dropped dramatically; in 1979, the proportion was over 60% but was 54% in 1980 and had languished at the 50% level or so ever since. The shift was from "middle-middle" to "lower middle." There is some justification in seeing this as the beginning of the breakdown of a sense of community in the Japanese culture, the most obvious cause being the rise in land prices.

The utopian perception of Japan as an almost completely egalitarian society is based on certain historical events. The Confucianist "class" distinction of samurai, farmers, artisans, and merchants was abolished in the late nineteenth century. Defeat in World War II wiped out the *zaibatsu* and militarist cliques. But more than that, it rests on the claim that higher education is equally accessible. However, clear and rigid status distinctions exist and are determined by the very education system that divides the members of the community by their status, such as employment in large versus small firms, and elite versus petty officials.

In the long-term, more than the short-term effects of land price increases, it is the strain of trying to attain the "right" status through the "appropriate" education that will start affecting the perception of equality. Such strains are already in ample view, with small tots attending cram schools and older children studying with private tutors. They add up to a mounting burden on the household budget; the emphasis on metropolitan education places a further burden on those who live outside the metropolitan area.

Equal opportunity for higher education has been the proud claim in Japan and the linchpin of a society based on meritocracy. Perhaps the subconscious feeling that the claim is less sustainable now has caused the shift in the "class" perception in the survey, as imprecise as the instrument of measurement may be.

As the postwar occupation had left this part of Japan pretty well intact—except for the removal of certain subjects that extolled Japanese nationalism—it may be that any change in the position and nature of education will, ultimately, have greater consequences on Japanese cultural values than anything since the Meiji Restoration.

An Emerging Class Structure?

Visitors to Tokyo these days never fail to be impressed by the Japanese consumers' visible expenditure on luxury goods. The strong yen and the weak dollar make the prices of most items here seem outrageous. The danger is to see this small island as being populated by opulent consumers, creating resentment in the rest of the world. As indeed, on paper, the Japanese are rich; in 1986, Japan ranked only behind Switzerland, the United States, and Norway in per capita GNP. Although official figures are not yet available for 1987, projection based on the current yen rate would pretty well put the Japanese at the top of the heap.

In 1986, they already occupied the most expensive homes in the world, although hardly comparable in size or quality to most homes in the other advanced economics. In calculations published in 1987 by the Economic Planning Agency, the total Japanese land value is said to be 2.5 times that of the entire United States, which has an area 25 times that of Japan. That means that the same amount of land in Japan costs, on the average, 62.5 times more than in the United States!

Enough has been written on the current uproar on land prices, so little more need be said. I would only add that the key threat is to the comfortable perception of Japan as an egalitarian, classless society, something that is cited by many Japanese commentators as the main reason for Japan's remarkable social stability and for the achievement orientation of its workers.

Still, the outside observer could argue that even if most citizens are now precluded from buying a home in the inner suburbs—without resorting to a two-generation loan—overseas travel is in the reach of practically all, and it is the value-added products that are booming in the market, so the Japanese are indeed happy spenders. However, evidence is hand that even in the consumer market a clear division is emerging between the have and the haves nots. This comes from the 1988 Ministry of Labor analysis of the "Trends in Household Expenditure," based on the Management and Coordination Agency's "Family Income and Expenditure Survey." Indications are that luxury spending is far from across the board but is much more narrowly based than expected.

When consumer expenditure between January and September of 1987 is examined, we find that it has grown only among the top fifth in income—by 4.6% over the previous year. Real income for this group grew by 3.6% over this period, so they spent more than the extra they received, suggesting a consumer group that is satisfied and confident. And lo! and behold, a miracle in Japan—with reduced savings! Even with no increase in liquidity, those with land may have just spent more because they felt richer. Presently, this means a reduction in savings, so the top-income group is moving marginally closer to their U.S. counterparts.

Against this, the picture is not nearly as rosy for the great bulk, some 80% of consumers. Their real income grew by an average of only 0.6% over the period, and their consumption expenditure, again on the average, actually declined by about 0.6%. So, while there is an emergence of a new group of high-spending consumers, with the expenditure gap between them and the rest is even wider than that for income. It is becoming increasingly apparent that Japan is finding it hard to maintain an egalitarian, middle-class society. While racial homogeneity can be preserved, Japan's renowned cultural homogeneity is already under challenge in the marketplace, which will result in very important shifts in intercultural societal values.

New Rich, New Poor: Are the Japanese Polarizing?

Polarization is a much discussed global megatrend. Businesses that do well are either integrated giants or boutiques—those in between usually get washed out. The same applies to products: it's either an expensive audio system or a cheap one. But does polarization apply to the consumer?

As noted, the Japanese have been advancing the theory that their high degree of dedication to work and social harmony is because, unlike in most advanced Western economies, there has been a lack of an economic class with the benefits of growth evenly distributed.

However, yet another new term, *nyū ritchi* (new rich), has crept into the Japanese lexicon, suggesting an economic class. (The Japanese New Rich are *not* quite the same as the Western *nouveaux riches*). On the polarization theory, this means that there will be a *nyū puā* (new poor) at the other end of the scale. The New Rich are currently easy to define: they are the owners of real estate and/or have made a killing on the stock market.

Black Monday has already begun to fade, and Japanese stocks are again reaching dizzying heights by the end of 1988, with Western price/earning ratios somewhat meaningless. Similarly, by Western logic, currently preposterous land prices should produce a large number of disillusioned citizens who will despair of ever owning a home on the rational calculation of yearly earnings versus loans. A 30- to 40-year pay-out for a modest inner-city apartment is an unbelievable ratio, but so are price/earnings of 20 to 30.

On the theory of an economic man who makes his decision based on price, this would mean that Japanese savings rates will at last start coming down, since, previously, saving for a home was the key motivating factor. But perhaps the renowned Japanese pessimism is just a cover for an innate optimism that fate will be ultimately kind, as there is still no evidence that the average Japanese is reducing his savings to spend now on the tangible versus saving for the unattainable. But, that killing on the stock market may help!

In the meantime, as noted above, the New Rich are busily cutting down on their savings. The paper value increase of their property creates a specter of disaster in terms of inheritance taxes, so they are naturally better off borrowing and reinvesting in amortizable business, thus reducing their net assets. An interesting study released by Nikkei in February shows that two-thirds of the landed rich are borrowing, and it is they who are fueling the consumption boom. The non-borrowers remain frugal as before.

How large is the New Rich segment? According to research by Nihon Shōhi Keizai Kenkyūsho (Institute for Consumer Economy

Research) released in January 1988, those with property assets valued at more than ¥100 million (as of January 1987) accounted for 6% of all households, the proportion doubling from the previous year. In other words, using this figure as an arbitrary dividing line, half the New Rich were created in one year!

Since land prices continued to rise, and although they show signs of a modest decline now, it can still be safely assumed that there were almost comparable additions by January 1988. So let's say 10% of the population is "rich." This may not appear significant at first, but this proportion of affluence is a substantial factor in the market. On the polarization theory, the 10% at the other end would comprise the "poor," and they are harder to define, if they exist at all.

Whether rich or poor, it is not the size of the category *per se*, but the rate of growth that swings the market. It then makes sense that in the retail sector, two growing segments are department stores and high-class boutiques that cater to the rich, and "discount" stores (including NIES shops), a euphemism for shops that sell Korean and Southeast Asian products, that cater to the price-conscious. At least the New Rich can be numbered; but if on Japanese assumption that the lower end of the scale hardly existed in any size before but has now emerged, then there is a gap that must be filled quickly.

On the "rich" end there is a fly in the ointment. Given that land price increases are tapering off, and that even the stock market must peak sometime, it would appear that the growth rate is going to slow down. But not necessarily, because the strong yen and the subsequent restructuring of the Japanese economy are creating a new sector of spenders, that is, a new class of entrepreneurs with a lower savings rate. Growth in mass production manufacturing in the past contributed to the middle bulge of wage earners who were not risk takers and kept saving. By definition, entrepreneurial types are more adventurous. To survive, they have to be creative and, thus, fuel developments in innovative products and services.

True, those engaged in exports are already suffering, but they have been more than compensated by those making money on imports. Again, importers are less tied to a rigid system of vertical relationships than manufacturing exporters and could create a more flexible consumer economy, contributing greatly to stimulation of consumer spending by breaking down price rigidity. I wonder if Japanese politicians actually realize what is happening to their consumer constituency?

"Kakusa" — A New Buzzword Triggers Debate on Narrowing the Gap

The seeds of the *nyū ritchi* have sprouted and a new buzzword is in the offing. It is *kakusa* ("differential" or "gap"). Like the previous buzzwords, it identifies pending organic change in Japanese society and, thus, is likely to be examined and debated with great intensity. Unlike *shinjinrui*, which was more or less a media creation, the new potential buzzword, *kakusa*, is like *kokusaika* (internationalization) in that it was thrown into the ring from the top, i.e., the government. The Maekawa Report, at first thought by many in the West to be the usual official Japanese window dressing, really got the ball rolling on "internationalization."

In this case it was the *Kokumin Keizai Hakusho* ("The White Paper on National Life") issued in November 1988 by the Economic Planning Agency. Japan must be one of the few nations in the world where the free press dramatize the dry prose of government white papers; the state-controlled press, of course, has no choice. Evening papers are generally filled with newsy events and culture-related features, with the morning editions tackling the serious economic and political issues. But, with the release of the White Paper, none of the leading papers were prepared to wait for the morning and four out of five gave it the lead position in their evening editions.

All reports blazed the word *kakusa* (gap) in their headlines, either highlighting the "accelerating feeling of unfairness," or "the retreat from the middle class identification." The impact of the perception of *kakusa* is not restricted to the local real estate market. The government white paper has clearly posed the issue in international terms. If we take into account the enormous gap in the prices of daily consumption items in comparison to many other advanced economies, are Japanese consumers really wealthy? Similarly, are they actually "wealthy" when there is such an international discrepancy in leisure time in which to spend what they earn? Is the tremendous gap in the consumer's saving rate between Japanese and the rest of the advanced economies due to ethical or financial reasons? Or, to put it another way, do the Japanese save because they like to or because they have to?

Kakusa (gap) is therefore strongly linked to *kokusaika* (internationalization) and the inexorable forces will be toward narrowing the international gap. Consider some of the implications on the market. The distribution system will be affected with modifications to the law that restricts the operations of large outlets in order to protect the small stores and keep prices high. The imports from NIES (Newly Industrialized Economies) will continue to increase as it becomes less viable to protect items with high labor content. Certainly, gaps in individual wealth are likely to widen, but increasingly, Japanese consumers will refuse to accept that they are the richest in the world so long as they obviously lag in many aspects and opportunities from their counterparts in other societies.

JAPANESE DISTRIBUTION:
GETTING CREATIVE AT LAST

Light at the End of the Tunnel?

HOW MANY ARTICLES have been written about the Japanese distribution system, not to mention references to it as the prime non-tariff barrier? Nobody can keep count because they have been appearing for more than twenty years. Unfortunately, most of them are dull; I personally do not want to see another chart showing inter-linking trading companies, A-to-Z class wholesalers, supermarkets, and mom-and-pop stores. It's enough to drive any marketer back to Witchita or Waga Waga, with the reinforced conviction that the Japanese market is just not worth the bother.

In most of the writings, the human element is almost totally eliminated, but distribution is the most human of all systems. I guess part of it is due to the fact that those who tackle the system are hands-on people who are engaged in sales and have little time for going into print. Many of those who write about it have never made a personal call to a wholesaler or a retailer—not that one has to be a practitioner to write about something; there would be few music critics or management gurus left, if we insisted on that. Still, it is more important to understand the people that operate the system than the charts.

This was driven home by Dirk Vaubel, president of a Tokyo-based consultancy firm, at a Marketing Breakfast Series for the American Chamber of Commerce. He was Chairman of the Board of Wella, and its success story in Japan is best told by him. However, one thing he said must be repeated since it demolishes some of the nonsense about this subject. " 'When in Rome, do as the Romans do,' " he said, "is all very well, but the Romans do it better." He went on to say how Wella went about looking for the difference they could offer to the Japanese wholesaler to create a niche. The Japanese game of "we are different!" was turned to advantage for an imaginative Western marketer. "Don't fight'em, join'em."

To survive, this has been the only attitude to take for a foreign marketer. It is a bone of contention and, at a seminar organized by the International University in 1986, Glen Fukushima, the U.S. trade negotiator, complained that the "Japanese definition of fair trade is different from that of the U.S." In Japan, fair trade means "no discrimination," whereas in the U.S., it means "equal opportunity." By the U.S. values, you could never have a sumo match between the Samoan-Hawaiian behemoth, Konishiki, and Terao, who weighs less than half. A featherweight does not enter the same ring as a heavy weight in the West, but he does in Japanese sports. (Until it became an international event, there were no weight classifications in judo, either). There is no discrimination, whether you are big or small; the former does have an advantage, though, so opportunities are not equal. Most of us that survived in this market have found that opportunities were not equal at the beginning because we were relatively small and, more importantly, we were newcomers. The situation would have been not too different for comparable Japanese companies—in fact, in some cases, being foreign may have been an advantage by offering something different. Certainly, in the distribution system, the "non-discrimination," "unequal opportunity" rule applies.

Also at the breakfast session, Michael Golding, the President of Franklin Mint Japan, forcefully put the case for direct marketing. Alas, the Japanese postal rates are among the highest in the world for bulk, and this, and the lack of decent lists, have held back the activity of direct marketers in this country. Thus, the inhibitor is not cultural values, although it has been said that direct marketing in Japan won't catch on because the Japanese are different—here we go again! Japanese housewives love shopping every day; there is a shop around every corner to fill the needs of most urban households, so who needs direct marketing?

In my pre–World War II childhood in suburban Tokyo, my mother did most of her shopping from home, although she was not Japanese; so did her Japanese friends. We had a *goyokiki* (order taker) entrance, and the butcher, greengrocer, and tofu man, all came to this door. Most of the delivery market collapsed with the postwar labor shortage, but until then there was certainly no cultural resistance to shopping at home. We still have the laundry man coming along in 1988 Tokyo, and deliverers are just a phone call away for bottles of beer, sushi, etc. Retail stores' share will surely decline as the *famikon* (family computer) generation find that there are even more interesting pastimes than shopping and start placing their orders through terminals. Marketers will find a way to provide the deliverers, human or otherwise.

But maybe we don't have to wait that long. With half the married women working and that meaning their having less time to shop, something is already happening. The news that the number of retailers has declined for the first time in twenty-three years is momentous, and the working housewife could further accelerate the trend. The 1985 commercial census shows that there are now 92,000 fewer retailers than three years ago—a drop of 5.4%. There is a commensurate reduction in the numbers employed and as distribution has been traditionally regarded as the shock absorber in employment, this too is significant. If this is a fundamental trend, we will start redrawing those distribution charts and the times ahead for the marketer will be far from boring.

It's Still a Long Tunnel

Overall, we are moving in the right direction Certainly, the long chain of wholesalers to the final retail store adds significantly to the cost of distribution, depriving the consumer of much of the advantage from economic growth, but before we get too excited we need to be reminded that even twenty years ago, there were those who said that this situation couldn't last; that the bulk of the wholesalers who employ less than ten workers would continually have their margins squeezed, resulting in a steady depletion in the ranks.

Yet almost fifteen years since the first oil shock, total wholesale value has increased by almost five times, exceeding the rate of GNP growth, which was slightly over four times. Past proponents of the demise of the wholesale trade, then, can hardly be labeled prophets. Still, with the pressure to internationalize, new expectations are aroused that at last the notorious Japanese distribution system will be streamlined.

It isn't as simple as that. With the restructuring of the manufacturing industry, a shift in employment—as has happened in the United States—to the service industry is expected. If that is the case, the existing service sector will have to absorb massive numbers of workers. It is true that the traditional mom-and-pop stores are disappearing, but convenience stores and small franchise fast-food outlets are springing up; the fragmentation of consumer tastes has meant good business for boutiques, so the net effect is only a marginal decrease in the total number of outlets. In other words, a large outflow of workers from the distribution sector will *not* occur. But what about wholesaling, then?

As long as there remains such a proliferation of retailers, the cost of distributing directly from the manufacturer's warehouse will exceed that of using wholesalers. So specialist wholesalers will survive, even if relatively small. Others are pooling resources while still retaining their identity and changing the nature of their business. For example, a group of forty-three wholesalers have invested in product development of household cleaning items from Taiwan. That means overseas purchasing forays, and ultimately they may prove to be a match for—or even better than—the large trading companies in introducing foreign products to the market. The trading companies still have to rely on the wholesalers, so at least one link in the imports chain is eliminated, hopefully reducing costs to the consumer.

But the most important development is that distribution no longer means putting something on the shelf. It is now essentially an information system and, to survive, wholesalers, as well as retailers, are in the process of undergoing rapid transformation. The Ministry of International Trade & Industry (MITI) is now encouraging wholesaling consortia to provide data processing services to retailers. Here is a new rationale for the distribution industry: the Japanese distribution industry will no longer be a chain of inventory points, passing goods along the line, but an information link between the manufacturer and the consumer. Therefore, it is premature to talk about the collapse of the wholesaling sector under the stress of internationalization. But there will be a transformation from an essentially feudal structure of personal relationships to a modern computer-based one, which provides instant access to relevant data. All in all, the distribution industry will continue to provide substantial employment.

Japan Plays by the Free Market Rules

Foreign observers are quick to ascribe various characteristics to the Japanese consumer, projected from their own preconceptions. In the March 1986 issue of *Tokyo Business Today,* I contested the contention of Senator Danforth from Missouri that the "Japanese had a mind-set that rejected foreign goods." I cited our own research to show that this was just not true. Still, whether there are foreign imports that are desired in sufficient quantities by the Japanese to reduce the current enormous trade surplus is a separate question. It could be argued that most of the major foreign consumer brands are already being manufactured here.

A famous Japanese professor on a panel in late 1987 asserted that there was little that the Japanese could buy from the United States to reduce the trade deficit. Calculations by many economists show this to be on the whole true. The currently raging debate on trade issues here makes one feel that the bilateral relationship with the U.S. is all that matters. However large and powerful as it is, the United States is not the entire world—and there are plenty of foreign products that the Japanese consumers could buy, given a fair chance. I pointed out to the eminent professor that every time I went overseas, I was continuously struck by the sight of Japanese tourists almost frantically buying up whatever they could lay their hands on. So if the price was right, there are many foreign things that the Japanese consumers would buy.

However, there is a school of thought that at least in their own market, the Japanese have a different perception of price. In an article in the September 1987 issue of the *Atlantic,* James Fallows writes that Japan is "not powerfully motivated by lower prices, because having more is not its principle goal. . . . Japan is not mainly interested in a higher standard of living for its people; America is." He was mainly talking about the producers rather than the consumer. He cites an Asahi Glass executive as saying that he would never leave his high-cost Japanese supplier, as they'd been friends in school. Still, if free trade is only viable in a world composed of "economic men," à la Adam Smith, who go through life making only rational cost-benefit decisions, even the United States would not qualify as a member of the free zone.

But the luxury of consumer nationalism is no longer tolerable for a country such as Japan, which has benefited so much from export. If you listen to some Japanese consumer representatives though, you would be led to believe that preference would naturally be given to local products either for national interest, rice being one case, or for higher safety standards, food, appliances, and toys in general. Leaving aside this contention, which I have discussed earlier, superficially it would seem true that the Japanese are less concerned with price than many of their Western counterparts, and that would indeed be an inhibitor to the free flow of goods, whose principle competitive weapon was price. For example, box stores—a concept imported from the West, in which only minimum service and primitive displays are provided in return for substantial discounts—flopped here, even though they opened during a recession. While the visitor may gain the impression that discount districts like Akihabara account for the bulk of electrical appliance sales, collectively the small neighborhood stores account for more. Here, clearly, the consumer is indicating the importance of service and a readiness to pay for it.

Perception of a lack of reliability has certainly been an important negative for some imports and in such cases price is not a factor in the purchase consideration. However, the fact of the matter is that for many imports, the price factor has never been put to a true test. Among price responsive American consumers, the newly industrialized economies (NIES) are emerging as formidable competitors to the Japanese in consumer durables ranging from cars to video cassette recorders (VCRs). If these items were given "free" entry to Japan, many could sell at almost half the price of the local product. Would there still be no potential for them?

The true test is whether the Japanese consumer would pay double the price for the perceived reliability of the local brand. Our research shows that the Japanese consumer would expect a price that was 30% or so below the local brand for low-ticket items from Taiwan, Korea, etc. Imports of various utility items from these sources have indeed increased rapidly in 1988 at roughly this price advantage over local brands. If prices were further lowered, the growth in sales could be explosive.

The critical test would be with relatively high-ticket items such as VCRs or CD players, for which quality and reliable service become the most important requirements. Typically, it is not import duties that prevent putting the NIES products in these categories to a fair test in the market place but the distribution infrastructure. Appliance retailers are generally tied to one or a few major manufacturers and therefore are precluded from handling these cheap imports. Even if that were not true, they could risk a boycott from the major brands. (Although this would be in contravention of the anti-trust law, pressures that are covert rather than overt can be and have been applied in the past.) In other words, it would seem that imports of electrical appliances are effectively prevented from reaching the bulk of Japanese consumers.

But the new consumers are getting increasingly wise to such ploys, and if the suppliers continue to act to protect the status quo the consumers have it within their power to play havoc with the current system. If the current retailers are not prepared to cater to an existing demand, new entrants will invariably find ways. An interesting recent case is the merchandising of NIES electrical appliances through the Tokuma bookstore chain. They already provide a corner for records and video rentals and now have added NIES electrical items. However, things have gone even further and the establishment of a chain of stores called "NIES Shop" has been announced. The first of these opened in Gifu in January 1988, and the number was expected to rise to 50 by May and 200 by October. It will then be possible to buy a VCR with recording and reproduction capabilities at roughly half the price of the cheapest local product. The Japanese chain is investing in maintenance facilities and vows to provide good after-sales service, meeting the reliability requirement of the consumer.

In perceiving that price was not a major consideration for the Japanese, together with other aspects, James Fallows argued that since the Japanese have their own rules, not in line with those of most of the free economies, they cannot be partners to free trade. In fact, his article was titled "Japan, Playing by Different Rules." He joins Peter Drucker *(Adversarial Trade)* and Karel van Wolfren *(Japan Problem)* in arguing for Japanese exclusion from the "free-world game.'' It would behove the Japanese government and producers to give consumers a much freer access to NIES products to prove that this is not the case.

Valentine's Day and Divorce:
Beginning and End of Romance

The Female Consumer: A Catalyst for Change

I HAVE OFTEN WRITTEN about the uniquely Japanese gift-giving custom of *o-seibo* and its impact on the market. Probably because of my ripely mature status, I have neglected that other ritual, St. Valentine's Day. Although not comparable in scale to the *o-seibo* season, for confectionery manufacturers it is a very important occasion. The practice was already going strong when I started my Japanese business activities in 1966, so it is not a new fad and is definitely here to stay, at least for the foreseeable future. I am not sure exactly when it started, but unlike the *o-seibo* and *o-chūgen* gift-giving customs, it is definitely of postwar vintage and was most likely started by some smart retailers to compensate for a dull period in business.

There are important aspects to Valentine's Day gift-giving that are worth noting. What amuses most Western observers is that in Japan, the female gives the male a gift of chocolates. I belong to the generation of Australians for whom Saturday night at the movies was an event of considerable social importance and a box of Red

Tulip or other brand-name chocolates for one's date was a must. Valentine's Day, as I recall it, was of no consequence for us "macho" Australians, and in any event receiving chocolates from one's girl friend would have caused some concerned comments about one's masculinity.

Here, not only does the girl take the initiative but she is getting very fussy with her choice. The major department stores always come up with an amazing assortment of items ranging far beyond the traditional chocolates and flowers. At the same time the Japanese single female is, like her elder sister or mother, a keen seeker of value-added items.

The *o-seibo* system is institutionally driven and thus more group-oriented than individual-oriented. Unless we argue that the concerted actions of the girls in February are just further manifestations of groupism, the Valentine's Day gift-giving is a very individual act. So the assertive female and the individualistic actions do not blend well with the conventional imagery of the demure Japanese female, and certainly not of the female beloved in many pulp fiction sold in airport stands. Surely, self-expression of this kind was anathema to the refined female of yore.

Actually, the custom that my generation had of giving flowers and chocolates to our girlfriends, always insisting on paying for the restaurant bill, stepping aside at the elevator, giving up one's seat to the ladies, etc., all originated from the condescension of the Victorian male to the female. The latter was the weaker sex, we were told, which had to be protected. The Japanese male, unaffected by Western romanticism, abrogated his power in the market when he conceitedly assigned the keeping of the house and hence the purse strings to the female. It was the male's role to bring home the bacon and the female's to cook it.

The Japanese male consumer, still very hierarchical in his attitudes, cannot hold a candle to his female counterpart when it comes to knowledge and savvy in spending money. The females have always been the more important segment for most consumer marketers, but they are getting so that we cannot take our eyes off them for fear of what they might do next.

Consistent with all this is another popular event that caught the headlines in January 1987. The great judo champion Yamashita announced his engagement, and the mass media was able to ferret out the event that led to his foresaking his single status, which was perfectly consistent with the other attacks launched on Valentine's Day. It turns out that he visited the Wako department store in Ginza to buy a shirt and caught the attention of his fiancee-to-be who was selling ties at the next counter. She was a great admirer of Yamashita-san and noted his address from the order he placed, sent photographs of herself, and the two started dating. What attracted headlines in the popular press was the manner in which Yamashita-san proposed. Fans were delighted to hear that, to his remark, "I'm going to England to study. Would you like to come along?" she replied sharply, "Just to England?" eliciting the response, "No, I want you to be with me for the rest of my life." Yes, he had formally proposed.

The episode has a touch of Victoriana and, like a scene from Jane Austen's novel, would hardly seem to warrant much popular excitement. Still, female initiative is the topic of the day. The market is full of females, unmarried and married, taking the initiative. In a recent study we found that middle-aged wives expressed their preference to go on a package tour with their girl friends rather than with their husbands. "He can't take time off, and besides it's a lot more fun with the girls." Half of the married females are now working.

While before the war, she only had a few years of her life left—larger families, shorter life expectancy—after her youngest child entered primary school; now, on the average, the Japanese woman can expect to live a further forty-five years, more than the pre–World War I male's life expectancy. The initiative displayed during the Valentine's Day season would be seen by Western feminists as yet another sign of the subservient role of the Japanese female. The equal opportunities law passed is rather toothless compared to the equivalent statutes in the West. However, the transformation of the female's new role is already manifesting itself in the market place, where her power lies. We are all watching with trepidation.

Divorce: Japanese Style

A man separated from his wife for over thirty years obtains a divorce. That is hardly headline news in most countries, but it was in Japan in 1987.

The man happened to be the "guilty" party, in that he had been living with another woman for all those years. In 1952, his application for divorce was rejected by the court, which declared that "the law cannot condone such immorality and selfishness." Japan has no religious strictures against divorce, so the issue is not one of sex but of social responsibility.

Even in the West in the past, only the wronged could sue for divorce. But for the most part, this stance has been eased, the argument being that it is pointless to enforce undesired cohabitation. Now, thirty-five years later, a majority on a Japanese bench has overturned the earlier decision against such a stance. Can we conclude, then, that there has been a fundamental change in the attitude toward divorce and that Japan is becoming "Westernized"?

Not quite. The fact is that of the 160,000–170,000 divorces today, 90% have come about through the conferring of the parties. The rest are primarily handled through arbitration, and only the very exceptional cases go to court. The absolutist stance on wrongdoing, until now, meant that the offender could not get divorced through the courts. But more importantly, there is shame involved in the break-up of a family and one does not go public.

Reference to the notorious *mikudari han* (three-and-a-half lines—all that was necessary for a man to send his wife packing to her parents' home) littered earlier Japanese literature. Although now not as arbitrary, divorce is still initiated predominantly by the male in Japan, reflecting the social inequity between the sexes.

More females would divorce if they could. In a survey conducted by the Prime Minister's Office, 60% of the women respondents thought that a divorce could not be helped if the parties did not get along; the number exceeded 70% among females in their 20s.

However, Japanese women are ambivalent about the court's ruling that seems to make it easier for an offending party to obtain a divorce. They need not worry on this count. There will hardly be a stampede if one has to wait thirty years, and the court has made it quite clear that it was only this exceptionally long period of separation that contributed to its judgment.

Economic security is, of course, the real issue, and as long as women workers are paid only a fraction of what men earn, even in this day when more than half of all married women are working, women will be reluctant to allow a relaxation of the divorce law.

The proof is that when it is the woman who walks out, negotiated settlements are easily made. But against the offending male, this so-called protection is yielding women little. The current situation is that the "full-time housewife" obtains only one-fifth of the assets generated during the marriage. And the average amount awarded as "consolation money"—the official Japanese term—at arbitration is only between ¥5—6 million (about US$44,000 in May 1988).

The cautious change initiated by the court on divorce has triggered a much-needed debate on social and economic equity between the sexes. The ramifications will be much wider than the original intention.

Moving Toward a 50/50 Situation?

For a long time, the female has been the predominant force in the Japanese consumer market, creating a disparity in her favor in this area. On the other hand, there is now smaller disparity in some consumer markets, and, if anything, the female is becoming even more important.

Smoking, for example, has been largely a male preserve, but while there has been a slight decline in the number of male smokers in Japan, this has been balanced by an increase in the number of female smokers. A survey published in 1987 shows that another male bastion is crumbling. According to the Prime Minister's Office, the gap between the numbers of males and females in drinking alcohol—at least in incidence—is narrowing dramatically.

About three in five adults in Japan consume alcoholic beverages—mostly beer, whiskey, and saké—with the ratio between drinkers versus non-drinkers reversed in the last twenty years. In this period, the incidence of male drinkers, already a large base, increased by only 5% to reach 78%, but that of female drinkers jumped by 24% to 43%. Soon there will be as many female drinkers as there are female non-drinkers. Interestingly, the increase was not limited to the young, but was charted across the board. It should be noted that volume is still skewed much more toward the males. However, when I first started researching the Japanese alcoholic beverage market, we simply ignored the female consumer as inconsequential; this is no longer the case.

On the other hand, qualitatively, there is still an enormous difference. In the survey, the main reasons males gave for drinking were "to be reinvigorated" (50%) and "to solidify relationships between friends and colleagues" (44%), while for females, one reason clearly stood out: "to enjoy participating in the family circle" (52%), which is a euphemism for drinking with one's husband. So, those who market to the out-of-home sector (mainly bars) still concentrate on the male. As the male/female gap narrows, the males will drink more frequently at home and the females more out of the home. The current difference in the drinking patterns shows that the role distinction between the sexes still persists.

In a recent television symposium, a prominent Japanese commentator suggested that more American males should hand over their salaries to their wives as a remedy for the low U.S. savings rate. Now, the Western male joke is that it is the female who spends, so here surely is an East-West perception gap! In a survey conducted by the *Asahi Shimbun* in 1987, 50% of women and 60% of men perceived the male role as that of the "bread-winner" and the female role as one of a "housewife and mother," a very substantial drop from the corresponding figures for 1980, which were 70% and 80%, respectively. Therefore, the gap in the male/female role perception is narrowing.

Nevertheless, the consistent response over three surveys was that about 70% of males refused to consider working for a female.

Another unchanged figure represented the response to the question, "If you were born again, which sex would you rather be?" The overwhelming majority of males wanted to remain such, whereas only half of the females opted for their own sex.

Figures can easily deceive. For example, one in three Japanese workers is female, but the largest part of Japan's 16 million female workers are part-timers. Chinatsu Nakayama, a female ex-parliamentarian, was quoted in a Japanese newspaper in January 1988 as saying: "Males are absorbed into corporations and are steadily exhausted by the logic of the systems. Active females are still not on the side that shapes society. I do not foresee the outlook becoming any brighter." Still, as we can see, in some respects, the gap is narrowing.

PART SIX

"INTERNATIONALIZATION," "GLOBALIZATION," AND ALL THAT JAZZ

Why Japanese Consumers Are (Not) Becoming "Westernized"

THE QUESTION IN THE TITLE is rarely put to me, and I must admit that it is my own twist to a personal hang-up. In fact, what I hear often is the declamation, "Why! The Japanese are so Westernized!" I have been hearing it since 1965 and I still react to it. It is delivered in several ways. There is the tone of surprise that indicates that the utterer was expecting a somewhat more exotic species. If one is a traveler, there is disappointment. If one is a newly arrived business-man, there is a sense of relief. Then there is, at times, the tone of resentment: "Why have I been fed all this nonsense about the Japanese being so different?" The worst is the tone of challenge: "Now prove to me that they are different in any ways that matter!"

In my earlier days of working in Japan, when I tended to have the answers, there was always the temptation to respond quickly. It is fairly easy to respond to the specific example given on the manifesta-tion of "Westernization": you can either deny or disagree, while, in the latter case, perhaps making certain qualifications. Either way, the so-called Japan expert is expected to explain the reason for not agree-ing with the proposition and the easiest way out is to do what the average Japanese does—nod your head in response to the statement.

Now, we old Japan hands know that this does not necessarily mean agreement but that, in the Japanese context, it simply indicates that the statement has been heard and understood. In this simple act, there is already a chasm between the average Westerner and the Japanese, because, for Westerners, nodding the head means you assent. For the Westerner, a proposition's truth or falsity becomes the immediate issue, and the nod, if not used as an indication of at least a modicum of agreement, would be considered frivolous and insincere.

My own problem is that irrespective of the manner in which the proposition is put, I feel I am on the defensive. I do not want to be perceived as a person who is continuously telling people how different the Japanese are. I know perfectly well that in many cases similarities are more important than differences. But it is too much of a leap from understanding to say that since certain characteristics are shared with the Westerner, the Japanese are becoming Westernized. This is not even "Western" logic.

Is Similarities vs. Differences an Issue?

A Western friend who had worked in the same areas as I for more than ten years in Japan but had since returned to his home environment wrote, disagreeing with my emphasis. He had established a deservedly high reputation as a market researcher in Japan and, without a doubt, faced many situations similar to the ones I had during his sojourn. Referring to my book on the Japanese consumers, *From Bonsai to Levi's* (New York: New American Library, 1983), he said:

I found that for the newly arrived businessman in Japan at least, the best advice I could give him was to look for the similarities between the Japanese and his own marketplace, being careful to stress genuine similarities rather than apparent similarities. I found it *psychologically comforting;* and something to ease the culture shock, to reassure people that there were, in fact, *some* similarities, whereas to the uninitiated reader of your book, it could be a little off-putting to think that *all* was going to be totally "different." The philosophical point of view, and one really far too complex to go into in any detail, might be one for you to think upon.

Actually, I agree with him. In the concluding section of my book, I wrote: "It would be overstating the case to say that all Western products that have failed in the Japanese marketplace did so because the marketer went against basic cultural factors. The reasons for a product's failure are usually multifaceted and not accreditable to a single cause. . . . Overemphasizing differences can be counter-productive in that it can generate a defeatist attitude. A good marketer is not resentful of differences but adapts his approaches accordingly."

It is an issue I am forced to think about a lot; although it is *not* what my friend was referring to directly, I really feel that the confusion arises from equating "similarities" in certain preferences, attitudes, life styles, etc., and going on to label them all as examples of "Westernization." I have already noted that Robert Benchley said that there were two kinds of people—those who categorize people into two kinds and those who don't. At times it has seemed to me that there are two types of marketers (both in Japan and in the West)—those who categorize the Japanese consumer as Westernized and those who don't.

Modernization vs. Westernization

Still, this over-simplification of cultural factors is not unique to Japan. Many Europeans complain of their youths becoming "Americanized." Perhaps the Americans are the only ones who don't complain that certain segments of their population are becoming Anglicized, Germanized, Italianized, etc. The American cultural invasion of Europe, particularly after World War II, has led to many changes in product preferences and life styles. To the extent that the products originated in the U.S., perhaps the "Americanized" epithet is justified. Here is the crux of the matter. Since the Industrial Revolution started in ninteenth-century England, practically all *modern* products came from the West. Products do influence attitudes and manners and to a degree it was accurate to say, when seeing non-Westerners consuming these modern products, that they were becoming "Westernized"; some may now say that force was applied to transform many of these cultures. Unfortunately, much of it is associated with colonialism, and we know that there are some reactions against the life styles imposed on these terms.

Even in this historical context of equating modernization and Westernization, Japan tends to be different. While products influence life styles without constant exposure to the culture that gave birth to them, they evolve in peculiar ways. Japan's isolation from the rest of the world is well known—officially the 214 years between 1639 and 1853. The word *sakoku* (literally, closing the country) was coined by a Japanese interpreter of Dutch in 1801. In typical fashion, the Japanese tend to think this is a unique action, but such withdrawal as a defense against an aggressive alien culture occurred in many South Asian cultures, as well as in Chin dynasty China, Korea, and the Ryukyus (now Okinawa).

The fact remains that there are no advanced Western cultures that I know of that managed to close their doors to the rest of the world for such a lengthy period. The fact must be qualified in that the Japanese government was not against trade *per se* but only to the spiritual challenges that the traders posed toward traditional values. (American fast foods are now seen as destroying the traditional values of the society by some Europeans!) Unlike many cultures, the Japanese have generally not regarded material imports as a threat to their basic values. They have, however, been conscious of their effects on social styles.

Non-Acceptance of a Western Product—400 Years Ago

The author Noel Perrin, working in Japan during a sabbatical, stumbled on to a historical curiosity preceding the *sakoku* (the closing of Japan) that he wrote about in a small but interesting book, *Giving Up the Gun* (Boston: Godine, 1979). Perrin had noticed the fact that the Western gun, called the Tanegashima gun, after the island where it first landed, abruptly entered Japan and just as abruptly disappeared, at least for all intents and purposes as a weapon, for the two hundred odd years of *sakoku* (I am taking the strict definition of *sakoku*, but most take the period of 265 years of the Tokugawa rule). It is on record that the war lord Nobunaga Oda had placed an order for 500 Tanegashima guns to be made (in 1543), not long after the Portuguese sailors had left the first prototypes on the island, which were promptly duplicated. They were effective weapons, helping Nobunaga to achieve surprising military victories.

Perrin was impressed by the fact that the Japanese had done something that no other major culture had done in the history of technology—abandoning a more advanced weapon to go back to a more primitive one, the sword. It is symbolic that the last major incident in which the gun was used in Japan was to suppress the Christian uprising in Shimabara in Kyushu in 1637. The perceived challenge then was spiritual rather than technological, and this led directly to the closing of the country to Western influences. The initially successful entry of the gun, followed by its eventual demise, tempts one to draw analogies with the fate of some Western brands in more recent times.

Perrin was excited with the fate of the gun to such an extent that it led him to wonder whether it was not a salutary lesson for the modern world—the pessimism over destroying or reducing the nuclear arsenal could surely be countered by this historical example. Perrin, however, did not offer the reasons why, under the Tokugawa regime, the demand for the gun withered. He only says that "somehow guns did not sit well with the culture— and for once, it was decided to put culture first." But I must disagree; in the area of marketing, at least, culture is always put first.

An Ancient Product Withdrawal Traced to the Prevailing Institutional Values

It would be nice to think that the Tokugawa rulers had high motives for letting popularity of these relatively destructive weapons—at least compared with the sword—to atrophy. Alas, there were no high motives toward abandoning the gun. I would conjecture that the gun would have been awkward for the ruling Tokugawas. After all, the gun, in contrast to the sword, is a democratic weapon in that anybody who so wishes can acquire the skills to use it. Only members of the ruling *samurai* classes were allowed to carry swords, but a similar restriction could be placed on guns, so that was obviously not the point. (Gun control is still very strict in Japan). The real point was that it took years of training to become skilled in the use of a sword as an effective weapon to kill. (The highly exaggerated skills of the samurai swordsmen in TV dramas and movies can be discounted as fantasy). As the non-ruling class could not train in its use, it prevented effective uprisings. In other words, the sword was more suited to the values of a feudalistic society such as the one that prevailed in the Tokugawa period (1603—1868) than the democratic gun. It is not surprising that the United States, the most democratic of societies, suffers from a surfeit of guns.

The Tokugawa shogunate's wisdom of going back to the sword and abandoning the gun was demonstrated much later when the government was overthrown by the forces of Satsuma and Chōshū from the southern districts of Japan. Ironically, from the direction where the gun was last used in battle, mobile units composed of peasant forces harassed the government forces from the east and the re-emergence of the gun was an important factor. Essentially, the acceptance or non-acceptance of the gun had really little to do with the Westernization or otherwise of Japan, despite the fact that the gun was of Western origin. It was solidly based on prevailing institutional values.

Westernization and the Shakaijin

The foremost phenomenon that excites new visitors caught in the "Westernization" syndrome is kids in Harajuku and other hip suburbs of Tokyo, especially on a Sunday. They are out in full force, in their jeans and bobby socks, dancing in the streets to rock music, going into pizza parlors, or consuming Big Macs. "Why, they're no different from our kids!" It is often strongly expressed that these kids could not possibly "revert" to the ways of their parents and that their new values will be introduced to succeeding generations as they grow older and start bringing up their own kids and so on. True enough. Japan is not necessarily a tradition-bound society, as we all know, and has and will evolve new social values. Accordingly, there will be new products to meet the needs of the new consumers. Some will be of Western origin, some will not.

Now, the Harajuku kids at the moment tend to lead the Western marketer on a false trail, if he does not understand the *shakaijin* phenomenon. The kids are in a particular period of life when their behavior paterns tend to be atypical because they are not yet *shakaijin*. The word *shakaijin* translates as "social being" or "public person" and while it is in common use in Japanese, there is no strict equivalent in English. When does one become a *shakaijin*? Till recently, for a girl, when she gets married, and for a boy, when he gets a job. Now the latter is also true for a minority of girls—more and more the single most important organic change that is occurring in the market.

In Japan, most females marry between the ages of 22 and 27, but the average age is creeping upward as is the proportion of singles in the older age group. The average husband is three years older than his bride. Like many things in Japan, marriage is, for the majority, neatly programmed; one does what is expected and there should be no surprises. When we interview a girl a year or so before she's married, and then a year or so after she's married, as far as consumption of many of the products are concerned, you would think she was a different person. As indeed, she is—she is now a *shakjijin*. She has stopped wearing jeans, hopping out for a Big Mac, drinking certain soft drinks, wearing certain kinds of makeup, etc. The same applies to the male. The moment he gets a job in an office, that is, becomes a *shakaijin,* like his female counterpart, he stops wearing jeans or going to the movies; he gives up soft drinks and "graduates" to beer or even whiskey and water.

The *shakaijin* concept, along with its corollary of not being one, is a convenient social device. The arduous cramming that the Japanese school children have to go through to pass a succession of tests that will eventually qualify them for a university cannot be ignored in the formation of their social attitudes and in their orientation to groups—the latter because they spend proportionately more time away from home than their Western counterparts. It is more difficult to get into a good university than to graduate from it. Thus, once the hell of the entrance exams is over, there comes an unrepeatable twilight zone of freedom before once again entering a period of regimentation, when one becomes a *shakaijin.* Since college days are a carefree period, corporations do not expect their new recruits to be immediately effective. It did not matter until recently, because, under the life-time employment ethic, the corporations had plenty of time to train their new employees according to their own methods. Note that I have used the past tense; although when I first wrote this in the spring of 1984, I used the present tense. I am glad that I have the opportunity to update it, however, since the forces of globalization have suddenly overtaken the corporations and are profoundly affecting even the *shakaijin* mores.

Dokushin Kizoku *(The Aristocratic Singles)*

It makes sense that Japanese society is very tolerant and liberal toward these young people just before they become *shakjijin,* as they will come under quite strict sets of social constraints when they enter the ranks. A very active market with unique sets of products have grown up, from globe-trotting package tours to donuts, catering mostly to this segment, and in many cases they share the common factor of an image of release from the conventional environment. The distinctly Japanese nomenculature given to the segment is *dokushin kizoku,* which translates as "aristocratic singles." In other words, the non-*shakaijin* are the aristocrats of Japanese society because they are not as bound as their *shakaijin* brethren by many of the social norms. One must be very careful not to assume that habits displayed in this period of their lives will necessarily be transferred to later life. Their ostensibly "Western" behavior patterns must not be perceived as the eventual "Westernization" of Japan.

In fact, to be identified with the *dokushin kizoku* too strongly could be a kiss of death for a brand if it wants to grow across the board. Increasingly, it is realized that youth is a very distinct market segment. In the 1960s, a marketer of a certain foreign brand of Scotch whiskey (which shall remain unidentified) must have decided that the best way to achieve growth was to become popular with the young, early in their drinking life. Its ads featured a nubile young actress which certainly succeeded in commanding attention. Although it was successful in introducing scotch to the young, overall whiskey consumption increased with age. As the drinkers of the brand became *shakaijin* and responsible members of society, they switched to brands with more sedate images, more fitting to their perceived status in the community, and so the brand lost in the bulk of the market. This particular youth-oriented brand has languished, stuck in a narrow and nonprestigious niche, and the "nubile" advertising approach was dropped. Domestic whiskeys, with a much larger chunk of the market, could (and do) have a brand focused just to the young.

Some of the New Trends are Not From the West

While we are on the subject of alcoholic beverages, the fact that saké consumption has been on a steady decline—surpassed by beer quite some time ago with, until recently, faster growth being recorded by whiskey and a potential threat of greater wine sales in the future —could be considered as growing "Westernization" of Japanese drinking habits. Wrong again! In 1983—84, a most spectacular upset in this category was caused by a clear brew called *shōchū*—a distilled spirit that is most popular in the southernmost (excluding Okinawa) prefecture of Kagoshima but can be made anywhere and from anything—potatoes, barley, chestnuts, rice, buckwheat, sesame seeds, carrots, you name it. Inexpensiveness was given as the reason for its booming popularity, in the hard times, especially with the favored tax status given to the brew. However, price alone is never the sole reason for the acceptance of a product, and *shōchū* cashed in because it fit easily into the Japanese drinking culture. The oolong tea boom, at last peaking in 1987 (for leaves), is another example of a non-Western trend. In 1986, imports of Chinese tea, dominated by oolong, still chalked up a respectable 17% increase over the year before, with the growth over the previous three years being remarkable. The growth of the canned varieties have been explosive. Sales were only 150,000 cases in 1981 but totaled 7 million cases in 1984, and the volume was 22 million cases in 1986, about 40% up on the year before. The 1-liter carton, sales of which totaled some 6 million cases in 1984 trebled to 18 million cases in 1986. Also, sales of bottles of tea, introduced in 1986, totaled some 3 million cases, and many manufacturers rushed in to take advantage of this category. It is estimated that there were over 200 brands of the canned variety in 1988.

What is my point? Simply that nobody is suggesting that the Japanese are turning Chinese because of their shift in preference for oolong tea. That would be silly, wouldn't it? Japan is currently not witnessing the observed trend toward white from red meats; on the contrary, it is reported that fish shops are having a bad time these days. However, as health consciousness continues to increase, there will be a trend away from the highly marbled Matsuzaka beef toward leaner beef, even without price considerations. The former can cost up to ¥10,000 for 100 g but this will not be the only factor that will restrict its growth. As in the United States, there will eventually be a trend away from fried chicken and toward the boiled form for the same reason—fewer calories and less cholesterol. One could argue that Americans are adopting Japanese dietary habits. All it means is that certain tendencies are shared among materially advanced cultures.

Let's drop the facile categorization of ''Westernization'' when dealing with other countries. Whether we are discussing the Japanese, Chinese, Korean, Thai, or any other non-European culture, the marketer should examine each culture and its country on its own merit and not on some perceived or preconceived similarity with the West.

ARE GLOBAL FORCES
EFFECTING ORGANIC CHANGES?

Globalization and the Sacred Cows of the Japanese Corporation

THE STEREOTYPICAL Japanese male office worker expects to be employed only once in his lifetime by one company, and hopes to progress up the ladder, devoting his entire energy to this end; throughout his career, he belongs to a company rather than to an industrial union or a professional group. "Lifetime employment," the "seniority system," and the "company union" are often quoted as the three sacred implements of a Japanese corporation. Actually, as far as I am concerned, there is only one that matters—"lifetime employment." If this ceases to be the case in a significant proportion of major corporations—staff turnover being already quite high in the smaller companies—then the seniority system will crumble and the company union, signifying devotion to the company, will become less viable. However, a survey conducted in the fall of 1987 by the Prime Minister's Office showed that the great majority of Japanese salaried men preferred this prevailing institutional arrangement, even if it meant sacrificing a certain amount of personal freedom. The outstanding example for the latter is *tanshin funin,* that is, being despatched to another area with forced separation from one's family. (Sixty-three percent of the executives interviewed in the survey said this was unavoidable.)

The Japanese have always displayed a reluctance toward organic change and have managed so far to contain change within the inorganic sphere. By this I mean that a typical change is effected in reponse to pressure from outside of Japan and that it is carefully orchestrated so that the basic societal infrastructure is not disturbed. Basic cultural values within the corporations seem to be the same as those which existed under the rule of the Tokugawa shogunate.

The current responses to the demands for so-called "internationalization" cannot, however, be classed in the same category as those in the past. For one, the macro-economic factors, most notably the rise in the value and power of the yen, are already producing a crack in the feudal structures of the manufacturing and finance worlds. With the former, a shift to overseas manufacturing is seriously threatening the vertical relations of subcontracting. When the feudal base is eroded, and the relatively fixed arrangements are disrupted, corporate values, for better or for worse, will be affected. These days, information and money both move almost instantaneously across borders, and an institutional rigidity that inhibits response will rapidly become nonviable if Japan is to retain a seat at the global economic table.

Although Japan is trying to cope with this situation without affecting fundamental values, the first of the three sacred cows, the seniority system, is being challenged. The feudal fiefdom of the Tokugawa period could be maintained through the sword, which was accessible only to the ruling samurai class. However, when the more democratic gun became readily available, elite samurai forces could be defeated by those composed of peasants. The old class structure went through a dramatic series of transitions. The entry of the computer into the corporate world is having the equivalent impact of the gun in a feudal society. That is to say, the ability to handle information through the computer probably has an inverse correlation with age: corporations are being forced to utilize "star" talents and to promote such individuals "before their time." The personal computer is a democratizing force that sees no national boundaries, and in this sense the Japanese male *shakaijin* (member of society) consumer is willy-nilly becoming part of a global information-oriented community.

WORKING FOR A JAPANESE COMPANY
AS A FOREIGNER

The Prime Minister Drops a Clangor and the Debate Continues

PRIME MINISTER NAKASONE'S remarks crediting Japan's superior performance over the United States to a racially homogenous society stirred up considerable comment in the Western press in 1986. I too joined in the fray—with some bias, since I am of mixed racial heritage—in a contribution to the *Wall Street Journal*, but which has already been covered in an earlier section, Part Five "The See-Saw of Change." Recent events have made the "purity" issue pertinent in another context. If the Japanese society continues to pride itself on its homogeneity, can a Japanese corporation become heterogeneous when it goes global? Two events brought the matter home to me.

We are an Unusual Company Because We Handle Foreigners and Japanese Differently

The first event took place when our company was featured in an

NHK (Japan Broadcasting Corporation) documentary entitled "The Day." The producer—in a novel attempt that didn't quite come off—interspersed real life episodes within a professionally enacted drama. The episode in which we appeared concerned the trials and tribulations of a fictitious Japanese company in establishing operations in Southeast Asia. Inevitably, we spent an enormous amount of time cooperating relative to the footage, but for television there is nothing uniquely Japanese about that.

Through my casual remark that we had a mixture of Japanese and foreigners in the company and that they came under separate personnel systems, the producer became excited and said that we may be ahead of the times. Our staff will no doubt chuckle over that one. The dual system—if you can dignify it with that description—came about only because of expediency. When we were even smaller than now, we operated under an essentially Western system of personnel management. As we grew bigger, this spelled nothing but trouble. So we hired a Japanese industrial relations consultant who installed an essentially Japanese system. It seems to work with our Japanese employees but would be untenable for our dozen or so foreigners. The NHK program included interviews with some of our foreign staff who had worked for a Japanese company before and who quite candidly stated that they did not want to do so again.

As a result of this appearance, I received an invitation from a major trading company to address its Board of Directors. This was surprising, because I thought if anybody knew how to operate internationally, in all aspects, it would be such a corporation. One of the virtues of the Japanese culture is that nobody minds professing inadequate knowledge and that there is a constant desire to know more. This humility has held Japanese corporations in good stead; they knew little about quality control until an American called Deming—the most venerated name in Japanese manufacturing, with the most prestigeous prize named after him—introduced the concept. It was pretty obvious that I could contribute very little to this giant corporation's personnel management—but foreigners, as outsiders, are listened to very carefully and it was the president that deemed that the corporation should break out of a Japanese straitjacket.

The other event occurred soon after when I was invited to be a speaker at a seminar held at Shimoda—the port where Perry's original black ships appeared. Many resident foreigners like me are asked to speak to visiting businessmen often and, let's face it, we develop a set pattern. I knew this one was a little different but I still took down my standard kit. However, I should have been more careful in considering the different characteristics of the group, which consisted of foreigners working for overseas Japanese branches.

Consider just a few of the issues I inadvertently raised. First, upbringing during Japanese infancy determines the individual's perception of authority. In many cultures, you must make demands on authority to get anything; in Japan, you are supposed to trust the authority to do the right thing and, indeed, to many Japanese, social codes ensure that this will be the case. A Japanese employer generally takes a dim view of an employee who approaches him with individual demands.

Then, the hierarchical Japanese personnel system is a natural outcome of societal values and is much written about. Of course, performance is rewarded, but over time. A Japanese employee doesn't expect to be promoted quickly over another who has been with the company longer, just because he performed better. The Japanese employer does not look for a star but rather a consistent contributor to the organization. That's why Japanese employees work long hours and don't want to take holidays. They want to be consistently seen to be devoting their energy to the company's interests.

The strong Japanese group orientation is cultivated through the educational system and is unlikely to change overnight. The problem is that the group, by definition, takes a long time to enter. As a foreigner, you are an outsider, and so all the rules that apply to the Japanese don't necessarily apply to you. You may have to demand and negotiate unless you are confident that you have been admitted to the group. Also, they *may* be looking for a star. Foreign baseball players for Japanese teams are only considered on those conditions. So all the talk about Japanese personnel management may not apply to the foreign employee.

These issues are for the Japanese employers rather than for the foreign employees. As long as the perception of them as foreigners or outsiders persists, Japanese corporations will have trouble keeping good foreign staff for long. And to be truly international, that's a necessity.

Coping with the Homogeneity "Hang-Up"

In other words, like it or not, Japanese corporations will have to accommodate other cultures. Can the Japanese employees be prevented from "contamination" by other cultural values? Or are Japanese values thought to be so superior that corporations around the globe will come to adopt all of them? A "yes" to either question is unlikely. Successful globalization of Japanese companies will have serious long-term consequences on the Japanese corporate culture that will not be to the liking of all. For example, for the Japanese, can "mongrelizing" be allowed at the management level while preserving corporate purity? Of course, this would be a contradiction in terms and clearly not possible.

Anyway, is such a choice really necessary? What interested the NHK television producer in our smallish company—we are certainly not a Fortune 500—is that the Japanese and the foreigners are working side by side, essentially preserving their own values. Both participate in decision making, and our corporate culture is a mixed gruel of values from both Japan and the West. We are certainly not concerned about purity and the Japanese staff are obviously influenced by the Westerners and *vice versa*. I can't say that we are a model of efficiency, but at least we are not disintegrating. If one side tried to force its values on the other, we would disintegrate, and I have seen that happen in some joint ventures here. (In many of these cases, the blame could be shared by both the Japanese and the Westerners.) So, to be a successful global corporation, a company must have no homogeneity hang-ups, and that will be a major break from the prevailing state of affairs in most Japanese companies.

Global corporations not wedded to any particular national boundary seem to be the emerging trend, but this should not immediately lead to the conclusion that there will be a corresponding globalization of all markets, a view that is forcefully held in some circles, and which I shall discuss in the next section.

Can The Japanese Be Part of the Emerging World Middle Class?

Japan and the New Reality of Globalization of Markets

"The difference between the hedgehog and the fox . . . is that the fox knows a lot about a great many things, but the hedgehog knows everything about one great thing. . . . [Like the hedgehog] the global corporation looks to the nations of the world not for how they are different but for how they are alike." (Theodore Levitt, *The Marketing Imagination*, N.Y.: The Free Press, 1983, p.-28)

The Japanese have a phrase, *isseki o tōjiru,* which translates as "throwing a single stone," which means that somebody has had the courage to disturb the tranquility of the still water in the pond, causing a ripple that keeps extending throughout. Well, the person who threw the stone into the marketing pond was none other than Professor Theodore Levitt of Harvard. I felt therefore compelled to tackle this issue head-on at the time as one who has perhaps been strongly influenced by "trivial" regional differences; it also happens to impinge on the tiresome struggle of branch versus head office viewpoints, which is not a trivial matter for many of my colleagues.

Now, Levitt is the great conceptualizer in marketing; he is to marketing what Freud was to psychoanalysis and Keynes was to economics. I well remember the impact of his *Harvard Business Review* article on me when I was a mere marketing cadet, which introduced a new phrase, "the marketing concept." It is now a part of our professional lexicon. It is hard to imagine a time when there was no marketing concept, and yet the event was historically not so long ago. It was followed by another now familiar phrase, "the marketing mix." In a very short time, Levitt clarified the way in which we should look at our profession. So when Levitt's 1983 book contained a chapter entitled "The Globalization of Markets," the whole marketing world stood to attention and took note. Some immediately ran with the concept. The advertising industry was divided between those for and against, although I don't know how the numbers ultimately lined up. On the one hand, there were the Saatchis & Saatchis and the FCBs who subscribed to the idea; on the other, there were the Greys, who did not support it. Both sides pressed their viewpoints.

Willy-nilly, I was drawn into the controversy. At the Asia Advertising Congress in Seoul in 1985, I presented a paper entitled, "Intercultural Marketing—Beyond the Numbers." At the same congress, Ron Sugerman of McCann Erickson demonstrated that globalized advertising strategy has saved millions for his client, Coca Cola. Our papers certainly were not arguing on the same plane, but inevitably, as reported by *Advertising Age,* our viewpoints were seen as being diametrically opposed. Subsequently, both the *International Herald Tribune*—which is purported to take a globalist stance—and *Advertis-*

ing Age—which appeared to be sitting on the fence—reprinted my warnings on "Beware of the Japanese-Are-Becoming-Westernized Syndrome" which I have dealt ad nauseam in the earlier sections.

How can I have the audacity to question the viewpoints of the great Levitt? In fact, Professor Levitt was devastating. There were two strikes against me. Firstly, he said that "to deny that Japan's case fits the definition of global practices with glib references to certain facts . . . is to mistake a difference for a distinction." One strike. To Professor Levitt, all differences that were cited in this context were beside the point, unless they could be demonstrated to be real differences and not just distinctions. (Incidentally, in Japanese, it is difficult to distinguish the difference between the words "difference" and "distinction.") It made it very difficult to argue. Next, I belong to a profession which Professor Levitt appears to consider ponderous and unimaginative in its utterings. Two strikes—one more and I'm out. So I went back to his chapter and found that in the context of my day-to-day struggles in the Japanese market, I still had serious reservations with his basic propositions. As the American saying goes, I now have to "bite the bullet" and so this is how it went.

Proposition 1. Globalization is not a phenomenon that has just happened.

Professor Levitt opens his chapter with the statement, "A powerful force now drives the world toward a single converging commonality, and that force is technology." Actually, in modern history it is argued that technological innovations have changed the world (read "globe") in cycles of 50 to 60 years. The Industrial Revolution that started in England in the late eighteenth and early nineteenth centuries ushered in the mechanized loom and the steam engine; mid-to-later nineteenth century saw the introduction of the internal combustion engine, automobiles, wireless communication, the airplane, etc.; and the twentieth century has brought technological innovations that are almost too numerous to mention—T.V., herbicides, the jet, atomic energy, the computer, and so on.

It is undeniable that all of these technological wonders have changed the face of the world, and that micro-electronics, new materials, and bio-technology will usher in the next phase of change. So what is new? It is the pace in which this is occurring. Alvin Toffler's *The Third Wave* stressed the explosion of instant information, which Professor Levitt also recognizes as the force that is causing "a new commercial reality—the explosive emergence of global markets for globally standardized products, gigantic world-scale markets of previously unimagined magnitudes." But if it is only the speed that is the variant—brought about by faster communication—it is a relative matter and could hardly be posed as an absolute or "new" phenomenon. All of Japan fell over itself to modernize after the Meiji Restoration that started in the mid-nineteenth century, and that was some time ago.

Proposition 2.   Aspirations for modernity doesn't mean that all cultures want the same things.

Professor Levitt asserts that "the world's aspirations now level simultaneously outward and upward, with increasingly larger portions of its population greedily wanting the modernity to which they are so constantly exposed. . . . All parts of the world want the most advanced things that the most advanced sectors already have, and no longer will merely the same classes and types of goods and services satisfy them.'' The fact that this proposition can be easily misinterpreted is not Professor Levitt's fault.

Still, it does happen that somebody in the alcoholic beverages industry in the United States who triumphs in the "white" revolution, that is, the growth of drinks such as vodka and rum at the expense of the more traditional whiskeys, sees a great opportunity in Japan where the consumer is still stuck mainly with *saké*, whiskey, and beer. U.S. makers feel that traditional *saké* can be passed off as a has-been, a relic of the past, as the steady erosion of the market may indicate. Ignored in this scenario is the fact that Japanese alcoholic beverage consumption was traditionally "white"-based, namely *saké*. Anyway, despite efforts, neither vodka, gin, nor rum has made a dent in the market, but a recent phenomenon that temporarily shook the liquor industry was the emergence of *shōchū*, a clear distilled spirit that has existed as a cheap local brew for as long as *saké* has. If it is the "white" revolution, and I think we are simply applying a Western analogy here, it still hasn't helped vodka, gin, or rum. Any way the market for *shōchū* has since collapsed. Sure, Coca Cola has swept Japan, but you can't formulate a general proposition from particular incidences no matter how many there are, so long as there are enough that don't fit. At least, as I was taught in my Western context, that is not scientific reasoning.

Propostion 3.   The "global corporation" is one that has a specific technological advantage, which, however, may be transitory; others must struggle on with regional differences and many marketing successes are achieved with no overwhelming technological advantage.

Probably Professor Levitt's most challenging statement is this:

> Gone too, or going rapidly, are the accustomed differences in na-
> tional and regional preferences regarding product or service
> features. Now in all aspects the world levels up in all places to
> world-standard commonality. . . . This means the end of the
> multinational commercial world, and with it the end of the
> multinational corporation. The new reality is the globalization of
> markets, and with it the powerful materialization of the global
> corporation.

Cola was an innovation in the soft-drink market that has achieved
virtual global coverage. Where it has not penetrated a culture it is, in
many cases, because it has been artificially prevented from doing so or
because of the lack of financial means among the consumers. Again,
this is nothing new, as we can go back in history to the automobile
or the steamship. It is important to know, of course, that the
category as a genre has enormous potential that crosses cultural
boundaries, as it will certainly lead to economy of scale, which is, as
Professor Levitt stresses, a powerful weapon of offering a product at
lower cost. But there is the danger in assuming that this dominance,
so evident in the culture of its origin, can be automatically transferred. Coca Cola and Pepsi Cola are slugging it out toe-to-toe in the
United States. But in Japan, Coca Cola outsells Pepsi by 10 to 1.
Gillette suffers the same fate to Schick in the razor blade field and the
General Foods' range of coffee is ranked well behind Nestlé's: these
cases are a reversal of the U.S. situation, and there are no all-
encompassing "global" trends here. Yes, you might say the dominant brand entered the market substantially earlier than the weaker
brand and thus was able to pre-empt the market. In all the above

cases, however, that is not true. It can be said that in each case, a locally developed strategy won over the imported, "global" one.

It really does not help to know that all consumers in under-developed economies aspire to an automobile; the winner is the marketer that taps into the important perceptual dimensions of an automobile, which are assuredly different by not only stages of economic development but by cultural values. The catch-22 is that the automobile will eventually affect the cultural values, and what finally evolves may be very similar across cultures. But until this happens, a global strategy will be successful only by accident. Unfortunately, we can't wait for the stage in which a global strategy can be applied: once the market has stabilized with incumbent brands, it is often too late, or very costly, to enter.

Proposition 4.   In Japan, we are moving from a value-for-price marketing culture to a value-added culture.

The impetus for globalization of the market comes from the enormous economy afforded by standardization, that is, the advantage of low price will invariably give the global marketer an advantage over the multinational marketer. This was true in Henry Ford's day, too. Yet price advantage alone did not sustain Ford, and the attractions of design innovation saw the emergence of General Motors. In Japan, the advantage enjoyed by Daiei, Japan's largest supermarket chain, in low pricing suddenly eroded, and the best performing retailer in 1985–86 was the Seven-Eleven chain. Daiei and others have moved away from pure price positioning in order to recover lost ground.

Evidence abounds that the consumer is prepared to pay a little extra for either convenience or perceived quality or image. During the recession, it was the standardized, "economy"-based product categories that performed badly, but, barring an economic disaster, the consumer is seeking value-added products as the standard of living improves. This is, of course, not an argument against globalization, as indeed, the success of the Guccis and the BMWs indicates a world strategy at this end of the scale is working very well. The real danger to the U.S. auto industry is that whereas in the past it may have been the cheap end of the market that the Japanese and other imports attacked, price is becoming increasingly less of an issue.

Can we really say, as Professor Levitt does, that "everywhere everything gets more like everything else, as the world's preference structure gets pressed into homogenized commonality?" That is absolutely true in the case of undeveloped economies that are striving to catch up with the more advanced. On the other hand, once a certain level of affluence is reached, one tends to tire of the Model-T and starts experimenting with diversity. The movement into the Model-T stage and then to the next stage in Japan may have been too fast for us to be aware of this fact. At this level, it may be dangerous to assume that price/value is the primary force that propels this consumer culture.

Appropriate value, of course, is the key word, but it is a mixture of "price, quality, reliability, functionality, design, fashionability, etc." In an affluent society, the last two factors, at least, will remain culturally based and their importance *vis-à-vis* price will vary by product to product and in many cases the issue of globalization may be a moot point. In fact, it is Toffler's point that with the great advances in information technology, we can diversify and yet still be price-competitive. Robots can be programmed to perform a variety of functions that only marginally add to the cost, and yet this may be the margin that gives the consumer that perception of a product as being value-added. Standardization à la Henry Ford is no longer the name of the game.

Proposition 5.   We tend to project from our own environment.

It is certainly comforting to see Gucci, not only on the Champs Elysées but also on the Ginza. The availability of McDonald's all over Japan creates an even stronger impression. But the latter is an indication of Japanese desire for variety and this alone is not an indication that they are becoming homogenized into a global community. There are more sushi shops than hamburger restaurants, and there is no fear that McDonald's is going to destroy the sushi or noodle sector of the restaurant trade any more than the popularity among a certain segment of Americans for sushi is a threat to McDonald's in the United States.

But the Western eye is selective and tends to see the consumption of Western-origin products as an indication that "ancient differences in national tastes and preferences, in modes of doing business and the institution of commerce" are falling. Most of us who are doing business in Japan sometimes wish that this were true. I remember that only thirty years or so ago the best seller in Europe was a book called *The American Challenge,* in which it was argued that Europe had to adapt to the U.S. superiority in management and marketing, and indeed, the dollar was almighty then. More recently, several books on the Japanese management have been best sellers. Both are projections from the prevailing conditions and neither is wrong in that context. However, one should remember the relatively short time span between the American and the Japanese challenges. There is no guarantee that the Japanese challenge is going to stay a longer course.

Professor Levitt's own examples are subject to different interpretations depending on one's own circumstances. Take the case of Hoover—the famous British electric appliance maker—which he gives. The table that gives "consumer preferences to automatic washing machine features, by country" is all Western. I would make the obvious point that Japan in 1985 had yet to embrace the fully automatic washing machine or the dishwasher. Professor Levitt's central point is that force of standardization in production and the consequent lowering of price by Hoover was able to override national preferences. And yet, Pampers pioneered the Japanese disposable diapers market but had its market undercut by a local product, Moony, which was not cheaper but more expensive! Could it be that local factors were more powerful than Pampers' global strengths? And yet, Professor Levitt states, "no matter how good the execution of a country-customized product strategy would have been, it would certainly have been suboptimal, and probably a failure." The obsession with globalism can lead to the dismissing of local data as inconsequential and as the obtuse cries of market researchers.

That we tend to interpret in a way that fits our case—and I am first to plead guilty—is evidenced in Professor Levitt's remark that Revlon's "problem in Japan was not, as some have argued, that [they] didn't understand the Japanese market. The problem was ir-resolution and impatience." And yet the irresolution came from their not properly understanding Japanese cultural values and the impatience came from the intolerance in not accepting that there are other ways of doing things. To me it still is a matter of not understanding the Japanese market.

Professor Levitt cites Smith Kline's success with Contac 600 in Japan. I was involved in the initial research and examined its progress carefully when it was launched. The company's strategy of forming a Contac Kai (group) was not far-removed from those intimate groups run by their competitors such as Colgen Kowa. The pharmaceutical industry has far fewer wholesalers than the food industry and thus the approach used by Smith Kline was along traditional Japanese lines. What was new was that a foreign company was flexible enough to adopt this practice. When Professor Levitt says "this was accompanied by certain special daily contacts with the wholesalers and key retailers," this was far from "violation of established practice," but exactly what the Japanese companies are generally better at doing than their Western counterparts throughout the world.

I was privileged to be invited to a reception for Contac wholesalers held at a hotel with a superb golf course—a more Japanese affair one could not have observed. Komatsu, the agricultural machinery manufacturer, as Professor Levitt points out, was successful in the United States market because they were prepared to adapt to the local customs in distribution. Perhaps this is why the Japanese marketers seem to be relatively more successful recently than their American counterparts—they are more "relativist" and readily adapt. The West tends to believe in absolute principles and globalism seems to be one of them.

Professor Levitt argues that despite the persistent regional differences in the United States, there is persuasive evidence of the homogenizing character of American life. True enough. But I feel the United States is an exception rather than the rule, and it is going too far to say that "if a large nation can be so thoroughly homogenized by the [various] combative forces, then it is reasonable to suggest that commonality can also advance and thrive among disparate nations and regions.'' The tendency for an economically dominant power to assume that all the rest of the world would or should follow their example is not just limited to the Americans. The British had it and probably the Romans, too, in their heyday. European countries continue to struggle toward the forging of a Common Market, despite the fact that they have had even more time to do it than the U.S.

However, what struck me at the Asian Advertising Congress was the diversity of the delegates—and there were indeed distinctions and not just differences. As one delegate put it, certainly we all share universal values: we all love our children, we fear war and poverty, aspire to material comforts, and enjoy good food. But those parameters are far too broad for us to leap to the conclusion that the global middle class will all finish up accepting the same brands because of some universal criterion such as value-to-price relationship. If that were the case, we would have to write off some of the most successful brands that sell at a premium but in fact perform no better than a lower-priced competitor in a blind product test.

Proposition 6. Radical technological innovation and amelioration of scarcity has global implications: but most marketers are powerless to change habits ingrained in cultural values.

Those products that lend themselves to a global strategy are the most visible and exciting because they exert an important influence at the margin where, as Professor Levitt points out, the leverage for change is the greatest. Yet numercially they would seem to be in the minority, which is another way of saying that for most of us, ''globalization'' is a theory that cannot be applied in practice, which means that the theory fails its true test. Neither the cake mix nor breakfast cereals first made it in Japan, but Western soups became quite common on the Japanese breakfast table. (Almost twenty years after their introduction breakfast cereals are now making advances.) There are culturally based reasons for this. Perhaps we should *exclude* food and beverages from our argument as they are subject to preferences and Professor Levitt may say that I was only making glib references to certain facts. But where do we draw the line? Disposable diapers have been introduced to the Japanese market and the concept was truly global. But the globally dominant brand—although doing well—cannot claim to dominate, and this was because the pioneering "global" brand was subject to local preference and attitudes. This may be trivial from a conceptual point of view perhaps, but it is important for practical survival.

Is the fact that Levi's and Avon became successful in Japan after deviating from their global norm trivia for a "globalist"? To suggest that a theory that works very well for high-technology products or those that fill a scarcity or that are visible symbols of advance that can be fitted to all product categories seems to be committing another sort of sin: trying to fit the facts to a theory. I know of too many specific cases that adopted this theory only to rue the day as a result. The word hubris can be applied to a corporation that confuses the power of technological innovation to transform society with its own power. Even IBM has to operate within Japanese constraints, which are not all institutionally imposed.

Proposition 7.   Cultural barriers are different from political or institutional barriers.

Some Middle Eastern oil countries are socialist, some are monarchies, and some are republics, and this fact does not affect marketing theory. More important in the theoretic framework are cultural rather than institutional factors. The Shah of Iran found that a head-on clash with traditional values caused the defeat of "modernism." What may be historically inevitable in the long run is a philosophical and not a practical issue for an operating executive, whose first concern is survival. The concept of "global" marketing, like the inevitability of modernism, may create a false sense of security, but no head office—whether it be Western or Japanese—is likely to accept historical inevitability as a reason for lack of success *now*. This means, as Professor Levitt points out, conforming to local customs—Ramadan (the month of strict fasting) in Islamic cultures and the *Oseibo/Ochūgen* (winter/summer gift-giving) custom in Japan. These are dismissed in the West as a matter of execution—concepts travel but executions do not is the standard refrain now. But what if the "habit" of separating "execution" from "concept" is a Western one? Then this all too pat "rationalization" is subject to challenge.

In one of our focus groups, a Japanese housewife described a commercial that was executed in a manner very familiar to any American viewer, as "like somebody stepping into my living room with his shoes on." A greater social offense is not possible in the Japanese context. That is an example of "execution" not traveling. Or is it just that? Why is it that department stores dominate the Japanese gift market? The gift may be Lux soap but it has a different value to the receiver according to whether it comes from a prestigious department store or the local supermarket. In this case, the consumer is thinking, "If you are not prepared to go to a decent store to get my gift, then you can't think much of me." In the case of the commercial, she is saying that "a manufacturer who doesn't take the necessary care not to offend me can't be relied upon to be meticulous with his product." Style—or call it execution—assumes a heavier weight than the concept.

When faced with the situation, the Western marketer goes to enormous lengths to demonstrate that concept and execution can be separated. Many of his Japanese audiences are nonplussed. In the marketing context, we are not talking about something as simplistic as concept versus execution, and yet it is the want of our training that forces us to see things in this light. The philosophical underpinnings of the Western and Eastern cultures are so different that in the areas of marketing communication—or put simply, advertising—they cannot be ignored, unless, of course, Professor Levitt prefers to concentrate his thoughts on "globalization" in terms of the product only and not the brand. I would expect not, as then he would be ignoring his own concept of the "marketing mix" within which advertising is an important element.

Proposition 8. One factor for the Japanese success overseas was that they did not suffer from the Western hubris that all things had to be done their way.

Professor Levitt feels that only one thing explains the Japanese success overseas—that they are able to produce world-standardized lines that compete on the basis of appropriate value. It is almost a technology first argument and marketing simply follows. It is like going back to Henry Ford, when the economy of scale seemed to be all that mattered. In fact, Professor Levitt does quote Ford quite often. I seem to recall that General Motors surged past Ford at one time because consumers got tired of standardization, but I wonder if cultural standardization may not be a short-term phenomenon like the Model-T Ford for the advanced economies? Granted, price, and hence standardization, is the all powerful force in developing economies. In any event, the day is already here when "marginal" variations do not necessarily cause a significant jump in cost. As Professor Levitt points out, it is what happens at the margin that counts, and in the world of standardization, whoever manages to create the marginal differential is the winner. One of the early appeals of Japanese cars was not that they were all the same but that they offered a great variety of extras as compared with Detroit products.

Looking at some Western failures here, I have often been able to pinpoint the cause to the marketer's tendency to ignore local cultural factors on the assumption that what has worked in several other countries must surely apply. These may be differences and not distinctions. However, there is a distinction when the Japanese enter a foreign market: they know that their way does not apply and they tend to defer to local advice. They have never had the hubris that Westernization was equivalent to modernization—a handicap from which many Western marketers still suffer. Only yesterday, I saw a paper that seriously contended that Japanese teenagers' values were approaching those of Americans—just because some convergences were visible, totally ignoring numerous "differences" that are hardly inconsequential.

It is true, as Professor Levitt asserts, that the Japanese do not indulge in as much market research at home as their American conterparts. He uses this as a put-down on the market research conducted in Japan. The Japanese system of "networking," however, in a tightly knit community, made the approach to information gathering different. It is not true that the major Japanese corporations do not conduct market research overseas, but since this is my profession, I should not be too defensive about this issue. Professor Levitt himself quotes Henry Kissinger on the continued success of the Japanese: "What could be more effective than a society voracious in its collection of information, impervious to pressure and implacable in execution?" Well, perhaps it is a question of definition, but to me "collection of information on the market" is called market research. And it is done because Japanese are not believers in the immutable. Rather, it could be argued that, in the case of the Japanese, it is not a relentless drive toward globalization but a constant shifting of positions.

Conclusion.   For the marketer, it is not the generic impact of a product that is the real issue, but whether or not his brand survives in a particular market.

Of course, it is so much the better if the conquest is global. It is significant that Professor Levitt speaks of Coca Cola *and* Pepsi Cola in one breath—in which case he is referring to a product category rather than to brands. It does not help Pepsi to know that all cultures are susceptible to cola, when it is outsold by a ratio of 10 to 1 in Japan. In any event, if the Coca Cola and Pepsi Cola examples are supposed to illustrate a convergence of the world's taste in soft drinks, then why is it that this hasn't happened with beer, which has been around a lot longer and has an equal, if not greater, coverage. It will take some time yet, if ever, for an Australian to accept American beer. Specific cases do not make a rule one way or the other and are of little relevance if you are trying to market Guinness stout to the Japanese or the French. (The Malaysians love it.)

But as Professor Levitt points out, all my discourse simply shows up my practitioner's bias. Practitioners are overly concerned about the details of "how we did it" and tend to lose sight of the broad perspective. Professors deal with "truth." For advocates of these divergent interests to take pot shots at each other "diminishes rather than enhances their reputation." In dwelling on detail, one must not forget the "truth" that clearly emerges from Professor Levitt's analysis:

> The successful global corporation does not adjure customization or differentiation for the requirements of markets that differ in product preferences, spending patterns, shopping preferences, and institutional and legal arrangements. But the global coporation accepts and adjusts to these differences only reluctantly, only after relentlessly testing their immutability—after trying in various ways to circumvent and reshape them.

Perhaps it is, after all, not in direct conflict to my viewpoint in *From Bonsai to Levis's* that "overemphasizing differences can be counterproductive in that it can generate a defeatist attitude." Professor Levitt has deliberately challenged such negatism and redressed the balance. I think he would also agree with me that "a good marketer is not resentful of the differences but adapts his approaches accordingly."

However, I concluded my earlier book with a practititioner's bias (and perhaps narrowness?):

> You can be lucky, of course, by not bothering with cultural issues, but in most cases you will find a local competitor emerging who will take over the role as leader simply because he is better at basing his strategy on local values. Tariff barriers, visible or invisible, are not the only causes for a product's inability to penetrate the market

You see, the problem is that a company's survival depends on local acceptance of its brand, and the fact that the product category—be it disposable diapers or cola—can gain global acceptance doesn't really help. Will the Japanese consumer be part of the emerging "global" consumer market? With some brands yes, with others, no.

Globalization Affects Both the East & the West

So much for what I wrote in 1985. But quite distinct from the specifics of the market, global trends are also involved. Even in Japan, the trends are sometimes similar to the West. In a Washington, D.C. meeting of trend watchers from the U.S. and Europe in the fall of 1987, I noted that there were many common threads for the advanced economies that lead us to hypothesize on significant global trends.

Japan did not fit one perceived trend observed in the United States and Britain—that toward de-urbanization. It was said that Britain is fast moving toward the population distribution of 1867, and that Boston, Atlanta, and other medium-sized cities are becoming more vital than New York, Los Angeles, and Chicago. In this age of instant communication, it really doesn't matter where you reside, provided you have the necessary information infrastructure. However, Japan's consensus decision-making process has resulted in an incredible concentration of bureaucracy, business, and media in just one city, Tokyo, with no short-term signs of abatement. Naturally, the consequences are serious, and currently, the Japanese trend in this respect runs counter to that of the West.

In contrast, in working habits, the U.S. is moving toward Japan and vice versa! In Japan, there is top-down pressure for more leisure, signaled not just by the Maekawa Report but also through an enormous amount of media coverage. It appears that Americans are working more and increasing taking their holidays in bits—like the Japanese—diverging from the European pattern of taking them in lumps.

The Japanese are acting on their collective consciousness to deflect international criticism, while American choices are individualistic, with working couples—the majority—finding that being committed to their jobs requires shorter bursts of leave-taking together.

In their attitudes toward change, there would appear to be a congruence between the Japanese and Americans, who are fascinated with it, while the Europeans seem more cynical. However, there is an essential difference. Americans are optimists while the Japanese are pessimists. As a result, Americans borrow and spend, trusting in the future, while the Japanese, distrustful of the future, save and lend.

All of this shows that the nature of change is changing for everybody. We can no longer expect it to be initiated from one dominant source. Good business ideas have a universality that is not necessarily culturally related.

For example, there is a world-wide boom in franchising, and the Japanese have their own twists; you can argue that the sushi- or noodle-shop chains preceded McDonald's by quite a few years, when hamburgers were totally unknown in this part of the world. When audio books were reported recently as the new fad in the United States, the phenomena was being observed simultaneously in Japan, which has gone one further with video magazines.

So it is true that the same factors create booms in different markets and that, increasingly, they are global rather than regional phenomena, since information is transmitted almost instantaneously. But one American trend watcher expressed it well: "The trouble is that we get information when it is about to change.'' To rephrase an old cliché, there is nothing more outdated than yesterday's information. Data of any kind, market researchers note, can only be meaningfully interpreted now in the wider context of global social change. But it is a process of cross-fertilization that is very different from the original concept of the ''global market'' that presumed standardization through a dominant influence.

CONCLUSION

Before the Dawn

Is "Real" Kaikoku Upon Us?

THERE IS A JAPANESE WORD, *kaikoku*, which appears in the dictionary as "the opening of the country." The word was first coined when the black ships of Commodore Perry emerged off the coast of Shimoda and has been in spasmodic use since, but, of late, it has been taken up with a vengeance. The trauma of *kaikoku* was described in an epic novel, a modern classic by Toson Shimazaki, which was aptly titled *Yoake mae* [Before the Dawn] and first appeared in serialized form in 1929. Based on the life of his father, it traces the path of the hero Shōzō, a squire, in this turbulent period. Shōzō was a nationalist who burned with the belief that the foreigner should be turned away from Japanese shores. He was an ardent royalist and rejoiced when the emperor was returned to effective power by the Meiji Restoration, and Part One of the novel ends on this note.

After Perry, a selected number traveled overseas to see how the rest of the world ticked, and to bring back technology to save the country. Although there was a profusion of translated literature, only a handful of teachers and technicians trickled in, and to most, the West remained an abstract. Hardly *kaikoku* in the real sense. However, this was enough to send Shōzō into a frenzied desperation and to his ultimate death. The book remains a monument to the Japanese dilemma.

From around the Tokyo Olympics in 1964, the average citizen started to travel out of Japan. Rather than weakening, the perception of difference was strengthened, which spawned a host of *Nihonjin-ron*—treatises on the Japanese. The emergence of the "Japanese as unique" syndrome was hardly conducive to *kaikoku*. While Japan was seen as a developing state, this did not matter. Now, the world is not satisfied with a sigh, a shrug, and the cryptic statement, "Ah, but you don't understand; we are different." In the theory of free trade—a concept that has never been put into real practice any-where—all parties must abide by the same rules, so the cry from the West is, "Why can't you be more like us?" The current debate on how to reduce trade frictions has little to do with tariffs and macro-economic factors but on how far the Japanese will tolerate a change in their society. There are many Shōzōs still.

Nevertheless, the intensity of the debate suggests that "real" *kaikoku* is upon us. Both Perry and MacArthur—armed invaders who demanded a response—were easier to cope with than the challenge now, which is more abstract, requiring re-evaluation of social values. "Real" *kaikoku* is a threat to Japanologists as, one by one, sacred cows are being questioned.

In just one day (January 15, 1988), a major Japanese daily carried four items which are more profound in their impact than the front page news on the yen/dollar exchange rate or international terror-ism. The first came from none other than the august *Keizai Dōyūkai* (Japan Committee for Economic Development), who coolly gave as

their beginning of the year view that "we are witnessing the demise
of Japanese-style management." The committee said that "the company man was an anachronism" and "life-time employment should
be re-evaluated." Even Japan's renowned homogeneity or "purity"
hang-up was questioned, although the debate was still on admitting
Japanese outsiders into the company.

Then the editorial was headed, "There are 1.9 million ways of
thinking," the number referring to those who reached adulthood on
that day, which was "Adult's Day," a public holiday. It lamented
that there was no evidence that the young people were, to any extent, becoming individualistic in their behavior—the "everybody is
going to Hawaii" syndrome—and felt that the educational system
may be to blame. The editorial concluded that "individual thinking
vitalizes society. Historically, societies in which all were alike were
not happy ones."

A president of the largest Japanese food company declared in an interview that "of the two forces that are driving the market—gour-
met aspirations and convenience—the latter was even stronger." He
went on to say that "there were homes these days without a *hōchō* [a
traditional kitchen knife]." In a staggering deviation from the conventional *kaisha* (company) philosophy, he said that the days of going
after market share were over. "We must purge ourselves of the
mass-production mentality" he said, "and adjust to the reality of the
fragmentation of the consumers' tastes."

Finally, but not least, was an article on the emergence in Japan of
DINKs (Dual Income No Kids). A book has been published in
support of this state and is said to be doing well. The article quotes a
1987 survey by the Prime Minister's Office in which 40% of unmarried female respondents said that "if financially independent, they
would be quite happy to stay single"; over half wanted to continue

working after marriage. One of the co-authors of the book stated that: "DINK is not an ideology but a state of mind. Even if in the future, one of the parties [Note that he didn't say the male. *Author*] quit work or the couple had children, the life style will be maintained."

All in one day's newspaper work. Who said fundamental values don't change overnight? Hold it though; the "new" values are *not* going to be 100% Western; they are still going to have a Japanese twist.

The Desire to Revert

Shōzō of *Before the Dawn* was not just a traditionalist who rejected alien values, but was a revisionist who rejoiced in the return of power to the throne. There are modern day Shōzōs in high places. As I climbed into a Tokyo taxi one Friday, the driver said, "Well, he finally resigned." To any resident of Japan at that time, there would have been no doubt that he was referring to Mr. Okuno, the Director General of the National Land Agency, whose disclaimers on Japanese aggression in World War II created a furor among the ex-victims. "I can't figure out why a man like that made such statements in public," he went on to say. I concurred, but soon realized that the cabby was amazed that a veteran politician was spouting his *honne* (true feelings) rather than sticking to the usual *tatemae* (what is expected). "After all, the British and others did some bad things too," he continued. In other words, why should the Japanese be singled out as villains?

The difference between this outlook and that of the Austrians, for example, who have their own ongoing controversy concerning their president's role in World War II, is significant. Many Austrians are in effect saying that the aggressors were the Germans so there was no choice but to go along with them; the traditional passing of the buck. What Mr. Okuno and others have implied is that Japan was no worse than the earlier European invaders of the East and, therefore, the aggressor label in World War II does not fit at all. So, no buck to pass. It was this message that clearly got through to the taxi driver.

Since I am not a political pundit, and with all weighing in on the Okuno issue, there is little I can add to what has been said. Most of the discussion focuses on the obvious: validity of historical interpretation, which is, of course, quite easy to refute. However, the Okuno remarks are just the latest in a steady stream of bloopers by well-placed politicians that indicate an undercurrent that no trendwatcher can ignore. The billion dollar question is whether the spate of revisionist expressions are the last gasps of an old guard or part of a consistent effort to revert to traditional values.

A strong case can be made that education laid the foundation for the tragedies incurred in the Pacific during World War II, placing far too much emphasis on the uniqueness and the implied superiority of the Japanese culture. Japan's tremendous economic success has created a new danger in similarly linking it with cultural values, albeit true in part. It was the sweeping implication of "cultural homogeneity" as the cause for Japan's economic success that upset me earlier with Mr. Nakasone's remarks. On this logic, Japan ceases to be successful when values become heterogeneous. I simply don't buy that.

There is a strong tendency now to infer that when traditional values are involved—such as worshiping at Yasukuni Shrine or in historical portrayals in textbooks—it is no business of the outsider.

Neo-nationalistic members of the ruling party have come out in active support of Mr. Okuno in this respect. Interestingly, they fail to realize that "insider" groups that speak among themselves and behave according to "insider" rules pose an anachronism in this age of global information. The most dangerous of Mr. Okuno's thoughts was revealed as he was forced to resign when he complained that the media should have the national interest at heart when reporting. This has a familiar ring to those of us who remember the days preceding and during the Pacific War. Who defines national interest? Mind you, this is not just a Japanese failing. Irangate produced a colorful cast of Americans acting on self-defined "national interest."

Practically all the recent blunders by Japanese, from former Prime Minister Nakasone to other cabinet ministers, such as the former Minister of Education, Mr. Fujio, were taken up with alacrity by outsiders—often before Japanese opposition had time to form. What is remarkable is that some of those responsible for insensitive remarks (to his credit, Mr. Nakasone is not one of them) display great sensitivity toward criticism from outside, as if that were an offense in itself. With the popularity of the term "Japan bashing," many now feel put upon. Much of the feeling has culminated from calls for Japan to internationalize, with the pressure of the pace of change perceived as a threat to Japanese culture. For the most part, the Japanese do not openly indulge in criticism of others, so it is hard for them to avoid becoming overly defensive when they are criticized. So the danger of an emotional backlash is always inherent, as a few old-timers will remember.

As far as I know, there were no polls taken on Mr. Okuno's remarks and, anyway, I doubt whether any would be meaningful;

we are likely to get just the *tatemae* (expected) answers. However, it would indeed be instructive to learn if some agree with even a portion of his views. Tossing out so many angles on taboo subjects, the proportion of agreement—at least in parts—could be larger than expected. The longevity of Japan as a global economic and perhaps political leader might be measured against such results.

The Final Twist: Japan under the Threat of Dumping

While Japan struggles with many challenges to its societal values, macro-economic changes continue inexorably. Did anybody think that Japan would ever be the victim of dumping? I thought only the Americans and the Europeans complained about dumping, especially from Japan. Well, the day has come. The Japan Knitting Industry Association decided, in 1988, to charge Korean makers for dumping their products into Japan. At the same time, the Sanwa Bank's think tank came out with a forecast that the dramatic increase in imports from the NIES (Newly Industrialized Economies) will dampen Japan's continued prosperity. Substitute Japan for the U.S. and the NIES for Japan, and you get the U.S.-Japan scenario all over again.

The similarities do not end here. The Ministry of International Trade and Industry (MITI) sent a representative to Korea to urge "orderly exports" (shades of various U.S.-Japan issues: textiles under Nixon, voluntary automobile quotas under Carter, and semiconductors under Reagan, that last now being charged as a breach of GATT). For the U.S., inexpensive imports of textiles from Japan and other Asian sources progressed to other relatively cheaper durables such as transistor radios, but the financial risk of buying such "inferior" products was not great. But when the products were found to be surprisingly good, consumer initiative prevailed with a demand for higher ticket items, ultimately fulfilled with cars.

Some Western commentators have suspected that this pattern would not hold with Japan since Japanese consumers are nationalistic and do not largely base their decision on price. Wrong. They have been misled by self-styled Japanese consumer representatives who continuously preach to their constituents, the argument by Japanese industry being that foreign products are inferior, unsafe or not worthy of the fastidious Japanese consumer. The willingness of Japanese to pay extra for service has also been cited. This fueled the argument in the Western camp that since the Japanese consumer plays the game by different rules, free trade rules do not apply to Japan, thus, Japan should be excluded from the game. However, until now Japan has been like the airline that offers only first-class and business-class tickets to consumers who are not given the option of buying an economy-class ticket. The basic difference in class on airlines, of course, is service, but the consumer doesn't decide policy.

Most of the evidence so far suggests that Japanese consumers are no different from any others. Given a chance, they have started buying cheaper lingeries and other textile products from NIES sources. So currently Japan happens to be in the "Nixon phase," with a trade deficit in textiles which has occurred with dramatic suddenness, leaving the local industry screaming. If outlets are provided, many Japanese consumers will begin to take a chance on lower ticket durables; indeed, some already have. If they find that the quality is adequate, they may progress to higher ticket items. Therefore, if left to the free machinations of the market, the low ticket "durable phase" will come very rapidly and progress as far as possible to the "automobile phase" of the U.S. With a national policy of maintaining the competitive edge in high technology over the NIES, however, the "semiconductor phase" does not seem to be on the horizon.

The dike has hardly been breached yet, but the waves are beginning to pound. The real problem for Japan—and this is where the earlier similarities with the U.S. cease—is that there is a commitment to increase imports to reduce the enormous trade surplus and, on free trade principles, one is not supposed to pick and choose among categories. Also, with Japan's record of indiscriminate exports in the past, the argument for orderliness hardly holds. Although the Trade Bill in the U.S. was temporarily suspended in May 1988, due to the presidential veto, its introduction—albeit with some modifications—was inevitable. Japan, to forestall further protectionist moves, was in the forefront of those arguing for free trade. As one Japanese commentator put it, there is a Hamlet-like soliloquy emanating from MITI: "To be or not to be." Japan and "internationalization": like Shimazaki's *Before the Dawn,* it is a continuing saga, but the pace is accelerating.